INTEGRATING READING, WRITING, AND WORDS LESSONS

A THEMATIC APPROACH TO TEACHING IN BALANCED LITERACY CLASSROOMS

BY

**DOROTHY P. HALL,
MARIE C. DANIEL, AND
JEFFREY V. MAGLIO**

CARSON-DELLOSA PUBLISHING COMPANY, INC. • **GREENSBORO, NORTH CAROLINA**

DEDICATIONS

I would like to dedicate this book to my family of origin (Mother, Father, and my four sisters: Jeanne, Katherine, Frances, and Christine) and my present family (my husband Michael, two grown daughters Michelle and Suzanne, son-in-law Ryan, and my precious grandson Cooper Aidan Hunnicutt). Their support has meant so much over the past sixteen years.

—Dottie Hall

I would like to dedicate this book to the many people who mean so much to me. Thanks to my family for believing in me and supporting me. I especially want to thank them for letting me bounce ideas off of them while we were supposed to be on vacation at the beach. Thanks for keeping my books on your coffee tables even though you are not educators. Of course, I cannot forget my biggest fans, my grandparents. Their admiration means the world to me. Thanks to Mom for babysitting while I worked on this book. Thanks to Dottie and Jeff for working with me, helping me be a better teacher, and inspiring me to do my best. Lastly, I thank my dad who always said, "I'm proud of you."

—Marie Daniel

I would like to dedicate this book to my two wonderful children, Jessica and Alex. Thank you for giving me ideas for stories and understanding why Daddy was always on the computer. I hope this book will someday inspire you to work hard toward achieving all of your dreams.

—Jeff Maglio

CREDITS

Editor: Joey Bland

Layout Design: Lori Jackson

Inside Illustrations: Lori Jackson

Cover Design: Matthew Van Zomeren

Cover Photos: © 1999 EyeWire, Inc. All rights reserved & © Able Stock

TABLE OF CONTENTS

Introduction 4

Airplanes and Airports 9

Apples 16

Beach 25

Bike Riding 33

Camping 39

Cities 49

Going to the Dentist 56

Fish and Fishing 63

Gardening 72

Having a Pet 79

Moving 87

Museum Visit 94

Picnics 101

Playing on a Team 109

Rain 116

Sleeping Over 122

Snow 128

Vacation 136

Zoo 143

References 151

Metric Conversions 160

INTRODUCTION

In recent years, many elementary teachers have become increasingly aware of the quality of their students' learning when subjects and themes are taught in an integrated way. The purpose of this book is to help teachers integrate subjects and themes and to provide a guide for first-, second-, and third-grade teachers who want to integrate their curriculum using the Four-Blocks® framework. Or, teachers can simply integrate a topic or theme into their daily balanced reading, writing, and words (phonics) lessons. The idea of an integrated curriculum is not new. Some teachers were taught to do this in their education classes in the 1950s and 1960s. The theoretical foundation for an integrated curriculum can be found in student inquiry (Beyer, 1985; Costa, 1985), schema theory (Vygotsky, 1978; Bruner, 1986; and Wells, 1986), and the whole-language approach (Goodman, 1986). All of these theories lend support to the idea that using a thematic approach is a valuable and effective way to teach students.

WHY INTEGRATE?

Schema theory holds that a student's schema consists of mental representations of knowledge and that a student often faces cognitive challenges that cause changes in that schema (Vygotsky, 1978; Bruner, 1986; and Wells, 1986). Researchers who have studied the qualities of effective teachers, especially those who work with culturally diverse students, found that these teachers are able to communicate new knowledge as they effectively teach skills and strategies to their students and do so while engaging students in appropriate lessons and monitoring their progress. When necessary, these same teachers help students understand the content, as well as the skills.

Students generally fall into several categories of prior knowledge from none or very little to a large amount. It is the teacher's job to make specific instructional decisions based on what is discovered in the prior knowledge part of the lesson.

Children who do well in school often have background knowledge (schema) about what is being taught. This knowledge helps their learning. For example, if a teacher asks students to write about what they did on their summer vacations, those students who went somewhere (the beach, Disney World®, Canada, Cape Cod, a fireworks show on the Fourth of July, etc.) usually have something to tell about their vacations. They cannot wait to talk or write about what they did and what they saw. Those students with experiences look forward to the assignment! However, students who did not go anywhere have fewer experiences and may feel they have nothing to say or write about. These students do not look forward to writing about their summer vacations. Why? They have no background knowledge on the subject!

The same thing happens when students are asked to read text at school. The more a child knows about a subject (for example, farms), the easier it is to read about a farm or a story that takes place on a farm. Children who know something about farms will probably know the vocabulary, such as animal names, buildings, and equipment used on a farm. If they have never been to a farm or read about farms, they have no schema for what a farm looks like, what equipment farmers have and use, why they use that equipment, and what else happens on a farm. If a student lives on or near a farm, none of this vocabulary is new; it is second nature. If a child lives in or has visited a big city, the same thing is true. Urban children know about subways, taxis, elevators, escalators, and skyscrapers. Children who live in small cities, villages, rural areas, or on farms may not know about these things. The more students know about a topic, the more schema or background knowledge they have, and the easier it is for them to read, write, and learn about the topic. In this book, we hope to show teachers that by integrating their reading, writing, and words lessons around themes and topics, they will help all students learn more and become better readers and writers.

Teachers can help all students become more successful with new topics in science or social studies or in their reading lessons by reading aloud to them from books about the topic and planning guided reading lessons where the students will read and gain new knowledge about the topic. Teachers can also include Working with Words lessons—especially Making Words and Guess the Covered Words lessons using words from the topic instead of isolated word lessons—and ask students to write about the topic. If teachers do this, they can help their students with one of the biggest problems students face when asked to write—lack of knowledge about the subject.

BALANCED LITERACY THE FOUR-BLOCKS WAY

This book includes lessons for Self-Selected Reading, Guided Reading, Working with Words (phonics), and Writing, as well as interventions for activating prior knowledge. These interventions include: teaching vocabulary in the prereading or prewriting steps; providing vicarious experiences with teacher read-alouds; and introducing a framework that enables students to build appropriate background knowledge for independent reading or Self-Selected Reading. (The most complete source of information about the Four-Blocks® framework is *The Teacher's Guide to the Four Blocks*® by Cunningham, Hall, and Sigmon; Carson-Dellosa, 1999).

SELF-SELECTED READING

The Self-Selected Reading Block includes a teacher read-aloud. The teacher reads to the children from a wide range of literature—both fiction and nonfiction books—including books on the current theme. Next, children read "on their own levels" from a variety of materials, including the widest possible range of topics, genres, and levels. These materials will also include books about the current theme. While students read, the teacher conferences with one-fifth of the class each day. The Block usually ends with some students sharing their books with the class in a Reader's Chair format.

(Much more elaboration about the Self-Selected Reading Block can be found in *Self-Selected Reading the Four-Blocks® Way* by Cunningham, Hall, and Gambrell; Carson-Dellosa, 2002.)

The goals of the Self-Selected Reading Block are:

- to introduce children to all types of literature through the teacher read-aloud.

- to build intrinsic motivation for reading.

- to encourage and develop children's reading interests.

- to provide instructional-level reading.

In this book, there are 19 themes/topics. Each theme includes a Self-Selected Reading section with a list of books—fiction and nonfiction—for teacher read-alouds. These books can also be added to classroom libraries so that students can find books about the topics to read during Self-Selected Reading time. Hopefully, students will find books "on their own levels."

GUIDED READING

Guided Reading is the comprehension and oral reading fluency Block. Guided Reading lessons include a before-reading phase, a during-reading phase, and an after-reading phase. Depending on the text being read, the comprehension strategies being taught, and the reading levels of the children, the teacher uses a variety of before-, during-, and after-reading variations. Before reading, the teacher helps students build and access prior knowledge, make connections to personal experiences, learn essential vocabulary for comprehension of the text, make predictions, and set purposes for their reading. After reading, the teacher guides students to make

connections between new knowledge and what they knew before, follow up on predictions, and discuss what they learned and how they are becoming better readers by using reading strategies.

(For more about Guided Reading, see *Guided Reading the Four-Blocks® Way* by Cunningham, Hall, and Cunningham; Carson-Dellosa, 2000.)

The goals of the Guided Reading Block are:

- to teach comprehension skills and strategies.

- to develop students' oral reading fluency.

- to develop students' background knowledge, meaning vocabulary, and oral language.

- to teach children how to read all types of literature.

- to maintain students' motivation and self-confidence, even if they are struggling readers.

Reading can be defined as the process of constructing meaning from text. It is a process that involves a continuous interaction between a reader's prior knowledge and an author's intended message. The importance of prior knowledge for enhancing reading comprehension has been well established throughout professional literature (Anderson and Pearson, 1984; Tierney and Pearson, 1994). Our understanding of the significance of prior knowledge has its roots in schema theory, the notion that individuals develop a cognitive structure in their minds based on their many and varied experiences (Rumelhart, 1980). Since readers in any primary classroom come to the reading task with divergent knowledge and abilities, building their background knowledge—getting them to think about what they already know about a topic and then use that information to bridge the gap between what is known and unknown—is a time-honored way to improve comprehension when reading about topics and themes. Furthermore, research has shown that activating background knowledge prior to reading improves comprehension.

The Guided Reading lessons in this book are not based on Fountas and Pinnel's 1996 limited definition involving leveled readers and groups. We base our lessons on a broader definition of Guided Reading found in *The Literacy Dictionary* (Harris and Hodges, 1995): reading instruction in which the teacher provides the structure and purpose for reading and for responding to the material read.

Note: Most basal reading programs include Guided Reading lessons (Harris and Hodges, 1995). We have chosen stories and informational books that most children in the class can read. The suggested text may be hard for some readers, so we offer reading activities that give these students some support. We recommend Echo Reading or Partner Reading, especially if the teacher does not think the whole class can read the text independently.

WORKING WITH WORDS

In the Working with Words Block, children learn the letter-sound relationships that allow them to decode and spell a variety of words, and they learn to read and spell high-frequency words automatically. The first 10 minutes of this Block are given to reviewing Word Wall words. Students practice these new and old high-frequency words daily by looking at them, saying them, chanting the letters, writing the words, and self-correcting the words with the teacher.

The remaining 15–25 minutes of Working with Words time is given to phonics lessons that help children learn to decode and spell. A variety of lessons are provided on different days. Some of the most popular lessons are Rounding Up the Rhymes, Making Words, Reading/Writing Rhymes, Using Words You Know, Guess the Covered Word, and Word Sorting and Hunting.

(For grade-level specific descriptions of Working with Words lessons, see *Month-by-Month Phonics for First Grade*, Cunningham and Hall, Carson-Dellosa, 2003, 1997; *Month-by-Month Phonics for Second Grade*, Hall and Cunningham, Carson-Dellosa, 2003, 1998; and *Month-by-Month Phonics for Third Grade*, Cunningham and Hall, Carson-Dellosa, 2003, 1998.)

The goals of the Working with Words Block are:

- to teach students how to read and spell high-frequency words.

- to teach students how to decode and spell lots of other words using letter-sound relationships.

- to have students automatically and fluently use phonics and knowledge of high-frequency words while reading and writing.

This book includes Making Words and Guess the Covered Word lessons for all 19 themes. Rounding Up the Rhymes lessons are included for rhyming texts. Other Working with Words strategies are included where appropriate.

WRITING

The Writing Block includes instruction in both self-selected writing (children choose their topics and how they will write about them) and focused writing (children learn how to write particular types of writing on particular topics). Children are taught to use process writing to improve their first drafts so that they don't have to think of everything at one time. Process writing is carried out in Writers' Workshop fashion (Calkins, 1994). The Writing Block begins with an 8–10 minute mini-lesson, during which the teacher writes and models one or more things that writers do. Next, students do their own writing. On some days, they are writing first drafts. On other days, students are working with chosen pieces to eventually revise, edit, and publish those pieces. While students write, the teacher conferences with individuals or small groups to help them learn how to revise, edit, and publish. The Writing Block ends each day with Author's Chair as several students share works in progress or published pieces.

(For more about the Writing Block, see *Writing the Four-Blocks® Way* by Cunningham, Hall, and Cunningham; Carson-Dellosa, 2005.)

The goals of the Writing Block are:

- to have students view writing as a way of telling about things.

- to help all children write fluently.

- to teach students to apply grammar and mechanics to their own writing.

- to teach particular types of writing.

- to allow students to learn to read through writing.

- to maintain the motivation and self-confidence of all students, even if they are struggling writers.

This book includes one or more mini-lessons for the teacher to use during each theme. Each mini-lesson features a teacher-written example of a narrative or informational piece (sometimes both), depending on the topic. Different grade levels and different students will require teachers to make adjustments, but these mini-lesson ideas will help teachers think of appropriate strategies to model for each theme. Students are not required to write on the same topic as the teacher's mini-lesson topic unless the mini-lesson proceeds a focused writing lesson on that topic. The mini-lessons will give students ideas to write about during each theme. As students begin to write more, teachers often assign a topic for a "focused writing lesson" during a particular theme.

It has been a long time since teachers were asked to "just" teach reading, writing, and arithmetic. Today, teachers are asked to incorporate many areas of study (language arts, math, health, science, social studies, art, music, phonemic awareness, phonics, comprehension, writing, handwriting, spelling, etc.) into their classroom instruction. Teachers often wonder, *How can I teach it all, especially when some of my students do not have the necessary background knowledge?* The answer is, "Integrate!" Integration makes sense to students and helps them understand why they are learning to read and write—to learn!

AIRPLANES AND AIRPORTS

Flight is every child's passport to the world. Unfortunately, many children will never get to experience this mode of transportation. By reading and writing about this topic/theme, children can live vicariously through the experiences of others, break through cultural barriers, and travel to thrilling new places. Being exposed to this topic will also help students know what to expect if they ever do experience flight. Their trips will go more smoothly if students have some background knowledge about airports and what it is like to fly in an airplane. Flight can be an exhilarating experience, but airplanes are confining and most children are energetic. Staying quiet in the enclosed spaces of a plane for a long period of time can be hard. Knowing what to expect will help kids plan their own entertainment in case they ever experience flight in the future.

SELF-SELECTED READING

Books for teachers to read aloud and then put in book baskets or on shelves for Self-Selected Reading:

FICTION

Gila Monsters Meet You at the Airport by Marjorie Weinman Sharmat (Aladdin, 1990)
A New York City boy's preconceived notions of what life is like in the western United States make him dread his family's move there. Children from all parts of the country will be able to find humor in their own fears about new experiences (such as flying).

The Stupids Take Off by Harry G. Allard (Houghton Mifflin Company, 1993)
This endearing, loopy family escapes from boring Uncle Carbuncle's visit by taking off in their plane and dropping in on some other relatives.

Angela's Airplane by Robert Munsch (Annick Press, 1988)
Angela's father gets lost at the airport, and Angela ends up in the front of the plane. She cannot help herself and decides to push a few buttons. What happens next sends Angela on a daring adventure.

Lisa's Airplane Trip by Anne Gutman (Knopf Books for Young Readers, 2001)
Lisa the dog flies to meet her uncle in the United States. She enjoys food, a movie, and other passengers until she spills her orange juice. After a quick wash in the sink and a trip to the cockpit, she arrives in the United States squeaky clean.

© CARSON-DELLOSA • INTEGRATING READING, WRITING, AND WORDS LESSONS • CD-104194

Fluffy's Spring Vacation by Kate McMullan
(Rebound by Sagebrush, 2001)
Fluffy, the class guinea pig, spends spring
break with Emma. He escapes from two cats,
visits the hair salon, and takes a trip to
the airport.

Amelia and Eleanor Go for a Ride by Pam
Munoz Ryan (Scholastic, Inc., 1999)
This fictional retelling of a true story
describes the April 1933 night that aviatrix
Amelia Earhart and Eleanor Roosevelt left a
dinner party and, still in their evening gowns,
flew over Washington, D. C.

NONFICTION OR
INFORMATIONAL BOOKS

Using Math to Fly a Jumbo Jet by Wendy
and David Clemson (Gareth Stevens
Publishing, 2004)
This collection of charts, graphs, and color
photographs is packed with practical uses
for math skills! Problems posed include how
much weight the plane can carry, how much
fuel is needed, how much food is needed to
serve passengers, and more.

Pilots Fly Planes by Fay Robinson (Child's
World Inc., 1997)
Follow pilots (both male and female) as they
go through a typical day of flight preparation
and execution. Large, color photographs help
explain minimal text.

Airport by Byron Barton (HarperTrophy,
1987)
Airport explains what happens from the time
an airplane passenger arrives at an airport to
when the plane is in the air. This is a great
book for children who are getting ready to fly
for the first time.

Planes at the Airport by Peter Mandel
(Cartwheel, 2004)
Bright, engaging illustrations introduce
children to all types of planes with whimsical
names. Loud, urban "whirly-bird planes,"
rural "barely heard planes," in-the-gate
planes, and more seem to fly over the pages.

Airplanes by Lola Schaefer (Bridgestone
Books, 1999)
Readers will learn about the components of
planes and how they fly. Other interesting
facts include what early models were like.

Loading the Airplane by Leslie Pether
(National Geographic, 2001)
Explain the mystery of where luggage goes
with this book that explores conveyer belts,
carts, and trucks used to help people load and
unload travelers' bags.

Planes by Francesca Baines (Franklin Watts,
Ltd., 2001)
Journey into the world of science, history,
transportation, and technology with this book
and its see-through drawings of planes—
incredible flying machines.

AIRPLANES AND AIRPORTS

GUIDED READING

Airport by Byron Barton (HarperTrophy, 1987) is a good informational book for grades one and two.

BEFORE READING

Ask children to think about what they would pack in their suitcases if they were going on a trip on an airplane. What clothes, toys, book, etc., would they bring? Remember, each child's items must fit in one suitcase and a small carry-on bag. Ask students to tell the class about any places they have visited by traveling on an airplane and then locate the places on a map.

Introduce the new vocabulary by taking a picture walk through the book and pointing out vocabulary words and illustrations that have to do with airplanes and airports:

- airport
- suitcases
- cargo
- cockpit
- pilots
- control tower
- seat belt
- buckle
- flight attendant
- runway

DURING READING (THREE-RING CIRCUS)

For first-grade classes, read the book first in an Echo Reading format. Read a page and then have students become the echo, reading the same page after you. Next, divide the class into three groups and display the following on a chart or the board: Business Class (read with the teacher), Coach (read alone), and First Class (read with partners). After each group has read the text, students will make a list of five things they learned about airplanes or airports. Students will share their lists with the class.

AFTER READING

Ask students about their lists of things they learned about airplanes and airports from the book. Make a class list that might look like this:

Things We Learned about Airplanes and Airports

1. People come to the airport in cars and buses.

2. Suitcases go into the cargo hold.

3. Fuel tanks are inside the wings.

4. The cockpit is where the pilots fly the airplane.

5. The control tower tells the pilot when to leave.

6. Flight attendants help passengers.

7. Passengers must buckle their seat belts.

8. The plane takes off on a runway.

AIRPLANES AND AIRPORTS

WORKING WITH WORDS

MAKING WORDS

In these lessons, you dictate words, and students use small letter cards (or cut apart letter strips) to make these words. (The "secret" word is the last word made and uses all of the letters.) Next, lead students to sort the words for beginning sounds or spelling patterns. The final step is the transfer step. Have students use the sort patterns to decode and spell new words.

Making Words Letters: a, i, o, p, r, r, t ("secret" word: airport)

Make: it, at, or, rot, pot, pit/tip, rip, Pat/pat/tap, air, pair, trip, trap, part, port, roar, oar, airport

Sort: –it (it, pit); –at (at, pat); –ip (tip, rip, trip); –air (air, pair); –ap (tap, trap); –oar (oar, roar)

Transfer: spit, flat, flip, stair, strap, soar

Making Words Letters: a, e, i, u, c, s, s, t ("secret" word: suitcase)

Make: it, is, at, as, sit, sat, set, eat, ate, ace, cat, case, cast, seat, suit, cute, suitcase

Sort: –it (it, sit); –at (at, sat, cat); –eat (eat, seat)

Transfer: pit, brat, treat

Making Words Letters: a, e, i, l, m, n, r, t ("secret" word: terminal)

Make: at, rat/art/tar, rain, mart, lime, line, mine, time, tail, mail, nail, main, alert, train, trail, retail, retain, remain, mineral, terminal

Sort: –art (art, mart); –ime (lime, time); –ail (mail, tail, nail, trail, retail); –ain (main, rain, retain, remain, train)

Transfer: start, crime, snail, sprain

AIRPLANES AND AIRPORTS

GUESS THE COVERED WORD

Write the sentences below on an overhead transparency or piece of chart paper. Cover the bold word in each sentence with two, dark colored self-stick notes—one note to cover the "onset" (all of the consonants before the first vowel) and the other note to cover the "rime" (the rest of the word). Let students have four guesses and write these guesses on the transparency or chart paper. Then, uncover the onset. Let students guess again, if necessary. Students will use context clues, beginning letters (onsets), and word length to guess the covered words in these sentences.

AT THE AIRPORT

1. You have to check your **luggage** before getting on the airplane.

2. People are assigned their **seats** before boarding the plane.

3. The flight attendants serve **refreshments** during the flight.

4. I like to look at the **clouds** from my window.

5. I like to sit near the **front** of the airplane.

6. My dad is always the first one to **spot** me when I get off the plane.

WRITING

Children must learn many different styles of writing in elementary school. They should start by writing about things they know and then transition to writing personal narratives, letters, imaginative writing, and informational pieces. The best way to help students learn a new form of writing is to model that style of writing in a mini-lesson.

DAY 1

GETTING READY TO WRITE BY CREATING LISTS AND WEBS

Tell the class that they are getting ready to go on an imaginary airplane flight. The flight will be long, and they will need things to keep themselves entertained while they fly. Have students brainstorm a list of all of the different things they could put in their backpacks to keep them busy while on the flight. Write your own list of possibilities on a transparency. Then, tell students you will choose one item from your list that you think you must have for the flight. Write that item in the middle of a web on another transparency. Then, have each student choose one item from his list that he thinks he must have for the flight and write it in the middle of his web. Next, think of other words connected to your web topic and expand your web. Tell students that tomorrow you will write a story about your item using your web. Have students complete their webs around their chosen words.

DAY 2
WRITING A STORY

Model how to write a story by using your web. Begin by telling which item you have chosen to take on your airplane trip and what you will do with it while on the trip. Add events, details, and a conclusion to your story. Here is an example:

> Tomorrow, I am going to take a plane to my sister's house. It is going to be a long trip, and this morning, I put something in my backpack for the flight. I put a good book inside and zipped it up.

After the mini-lesson, students will follow the same procedure.

After they write their stories, have a few students share their pieces. Then, discuss how everyone started with the same idea, chose different items, and wrote different stories.

For a follow-up activity on the third day, the class can look at their papers and self-edit to add an imaginative spin. Tell students the items they put in their backpacks must be things that can "come to life" on the plane, such as an action figure or doll.

QUICK WRITES OR OTHER IDEAS FOR WRITING MINI-LESSONS

Here are a few Quick Writes that can be posted in the room so that children will have writing activities to work on. These ideas also could be used for other mini-lessons while learning about airplanes and airports.

- Write a story about meeting a friend at the airport.

- Write about a place you visited by plane.

- If you could fly to any place in the world, where would it be, and why would you go there?

FOOD ACTIVITY

PRETZELS

When you fly, you usually get a snack like pretzels and peanuts along with a soda, water, or juice. For this cooking activity, you can make homemade pretzels and serve them with a choice of beverages. (If you can't cook at your school, or you must used packaged snacks, serve small bags of pretzels instead of the homemade version.)

Caution: Before completing any food activity, ask families' permission and inquire about students' food allergies and religious or other food preferences.

AIRPLANES AND AIRPORTS

INGREDIENTS

- 2 tsp. dry yeast
- 1½ cups warm water
- 1½ tsp. salt
- 1 tsp. melted butter or vegetable oil

- 3½ cups unbleached white flour (or 2½ cups white and 1 cup whole wheat flour)
- 1 egg yolk

- 1 tsp. water
- 1 tbsp. sugar
- Coarse salt or poppy seeds (optional)

DIRECTIONS

1. Dissolve the yeast in the warm water in a mixing bowl. Add melted butter (or vegetable oil) and salt. Add one tablespoon of sugar to the mixture. This speeds up the yeast action so that the dough can be worked with no rising time required.

2. Stir in the flour with a spoon until it becomes too thick to stir. Put the dough onto a well-floured board and let it rest while you clean and oil the bowl. Briefly knead the dough. (Children will enjoy the kneading!) After kneading, roll the dough into approximately six snakelike portions and let students make whatever shapes they like.

3. Next, brush the pretzel shapes with a mixture of one beaten egg yolk and one teaspoon of water.

4. Finally, cover a cookie sheet with aluminum foil, shiny side down. Place the pretzels on the sheet and sprinkle them with coarse salt or poppy seeds. Bake for 15 minutes at 425°. Most cafeteria managers will be more than willing to cook things for you as long as you do the project early in the morning, so that the pretzels can finish baking before the mad dash to lunch begins.

CULMINATING ACTIVITY

VIEW FROM ABOVE

Let students build what they would see if they looked out of a window while flying in an airplane. Provide toy cars and let students draw roads and runways. They can use shoe boxes for airport buildings (hangars, towers, etc.) and cereal boxes for hotels and high-rises. Let students be creative and have fun.

© CARSON-DELLOSA • INTEGRATING READING, WRITING, AND WORDS LESSONS • CD-104194

APPLES

Fall is a great time to talk about apples and the popular American legend, Johnny Appleseed. Apples are grown in many areas of the United States and Canada. Young children can learn how apples grow, how apples are harvested, and what people make with apples. Children who live near apple orchards have more knowledge of apples than those children who only see them in grocery stores or at a neighborhood fruit stand. When teachers choose apples as a theme for reading and writing activities, they can help students gain more knowledge about this popular and healthy fruit.

SELF-SELECTED READING

Books for teachers to read aloud and then put in book baskets or on shelves for Self-Selected Reading:

FICTION

Apples, Apples, Apples by Nancy Elizabeth Wallace (Marshall Cavendish Corporation, 2004)
At Long Hill Orchard, a farmer takes a family on a tour and explains how apples are grown, the different colors and kinds of apples, and some interesting apple facts. Included are an apple recipe, instructions for how to make apple prints, and a song about apples.

Johnny Appleseed retold by Steven Kellogg (HarperCollins, 1988)
Kellogg retells the familiar tall tale of an American frontier hero named John Chapman—later called Johnny Appleseed—by sharing tales from Johnny's life and travels, complete with exaggerations and embellishments appropriate to the tall tale genre.

The Seasons of Arnold's Apple Tree by Gail Gibbons (Voyager Books, 1989)
Arnold's apple tree shows readers how a tree grows and changes through the seasons as Arnold grows up and changes.

Up, Up, Up! It's Apple-Picking Time by Jody Fickes Shapiro (Holiday House, 2003)
A family takes a trip to Grandpa and Granny's apple orchard for a wonderful day of picking, eating, and selling apples. The day ends with apple dumplings and a roaring fire.

NONFICTION OR INFORMATIONAL BOOKS

Apples by Gail Gibbons (Holiday House, 2000)
This book celebrates the life cycle of apples, how they grow, their parts, and their varieties. Gibbons explores their uses in juice, jelly, cider, pie, and more, as well as how to care for them.

Apples by Ken Robbins (Atheneum, 2002)
This informational book about apples uses photography to show what apples look like, how new trees are grafted, how people eat them, and more. Simple text delivers a variety of information.

Apples by Melvin and Gilda Berger (Scholastic, 2004)
This is an easy-to-read book filled with apple facts.

Apples Here! by Will Hubbell (Albert Whitman & Company, 2002)
Very brief text and beautiful illustrations make this book for young children a standout. Includes two pages of apple facts.

Fruit by Gallimard Jeanesse (Scholastic, Inc., 1991)
Different kinds of fruit, including apples, are showcased in this easy-to-read book.

The Apple Pie Tree by Zoe Hall (Blue Sky Press, 1996)
Paint-and-paper collage illustrations show the many uses of an apple tree, such as a supplier of apple pie fruit and a home for two birds.

How Do Apples Grow? by Betsy Maestro (HarperTrophy, 1993)
This easy-to-follow book details the life of an apple tree and apple growth from flower to fruit.

Apples and Pumpkins by Anne Rockwell (Aladdin, 1994)
A family takes a trip to Mr. Comstock's farm to partake in the fall harvest by gathering apples and pumpkins.

GUIDED READING: FICTION

Students in grade two (or three) may read *Johnny Appleseed* retold by Steven Kellogg (HarperCollins, 1988). In grade two, the text can be divided in half. It may be too much for second graders to read in one day (but not for students in grade three). There are no page numbers so tell students to read to the middle of the book or put a paper clip in the middle of the book and tell students to read to it. Then, have students finish the book on the second day.

DAY 1
BEFORE READING

Talk about tall tales and how people often exaggerate the deeds they have done. See if students know about the pioneers, the American frontier, and what life was like long ago. Ask students if they know anything about Johnny Appleseed or the apple orchards he planted. Tell students they will begin to read a tall tale about a popular American frontier hero who lived long ago. As they are reading, they should decide what they think is true and what is exaggerated. You might do a Rivet lesson (page 26) with some of the important vocabulary words—tall tales, exaggerate, pioneers, frontier, orchards, etc.—and then make some predictions before students begin to read the story.

DURING READING (PARTNER READING)

Students will read the book with partners, and the partners will take turns reading one page at a time. There are some pages in this book with just pictures and no print to read. Be sure to tell students what to do when they get to a page with only a picture: look at the picture on the page, see what is happening, tell their partners if they see something interesting, and then go to the next page. After each page, have students stop, think, and tell whether the page is true or exaggerated. Model the first page for students. (Read the first page aloud, stop, pretend you are thinking, and then tell students you think the page is true because you know Johnny Appleseed's real name was John Chapman, and you know he was born in Massachusetts.) Begin a chart that lists the real facts and the exaggerated statements you found on the first pages.

Real	Exaggerated
Johnny Appleseed's real name was John Chapman.	

AFTER READING

Call on children to read each page out loud and tell if the information on the page is real or exaggerated. Write the information on the Real/Exaggerated Chart in the correct columns.

DAY 2
BEFORE READING

Discuss what has happened in this story so far and how most of it describes true facts about Johnny Appleseed. Let students predict whether what they will be reading in the second part of the book will be mostly true or exaggerated.

DURING READING (PARTNER READING)

Have students read the second half of the book with partners; partners will take turns reading one page at a time. After each page, have students stop, think, and tell whether the page is true or exaggerated. Model the first page in this section for students.

(Read the first page in this section out loud, stop, pretend you are thinking, and then tell students you think the page is true because people did call John Chapman by the name Johnny Appleseed.)

AFTER READING

After students have read the second part and told their partners which events they think are true and which events they think are exaggerated, call on students to read each page out loud and tell if the information on the page is real or exaggerated. Continue to fill in the Real/Exaggerated Chart you started on Day One. Finally, ask students, "Did the second part of the book have more real events or more exaggerated events? How do you know?"

GUIDED READING: NONFICTION

Students in second and third grade can also read the informational book *Apples* by Ken Robbins (Atheneum, 2002). There are numbers on the pages, so tell students how many pages they will read (the whole book or just a part of it) and if they will read with partners or by themselves.

DAY 1
BEFORE READING

Make a KWL Chart and list in the K column all of the things students **K**now about apples, such as how they grow and what people make with them. You can also fill in the W column listing things students **W**ant to learn or **W**onder about apples.

DURING READING (INDEPENDENT, PARTNER, OR ECHO READING)

Have students read to page 28 by themselves, with partners, or Echo Reading with you depending on how much support they need. If students are Partner Reading or reading by themselves, give them self-stick notes to put on pages and have them write facts as they learn them. Circulate among students and help as needed.

AFTER READING

Let students make a list of things they **L**earned in this book. Their self-stick notes should help them remember these facts.

DAY 2
BEFORE READING

Review what students **K**new, **W**ondered, and **L**earned about apples while reading this book. Then, tell them the author has even more to tell them about apples on pages 30–31. And, don't forget the list of common apple types on page 32.

DURING READING (INDEPENDENT OR WITH A PARTNER)

Today's pages can be read alone or with partners, but there is too much text for Echo Reading. If students find the text difficult and are not capable of reading it by themselves, then choose an easier book.*

AFTER READING

Draw and write. Have each student draw a picture of something she learned about apples and write a sentence about it.

Apples by Melvin and Gilda Berger (Scholastic, 2004) is an easier text that can be used with first graders and some second-grade classes. Children can Echo Read or read after the teacher, and the same before and after format (KWL) found in the above lesson can be used.

WORKING WITH WORDS

MAKING WORDS

In these lessons, you dictate words, and students use small letter cards (or cut apart letter strips) to make these words. (The "secret" word is the last word made and uses all of the letters.) Next, lead students to sort the words for beginning sounds or spelling patterns. The final step is the transfer step. Have students use the sort patterns to decode and spell new words.

Making Words Letters: a, e, l, p, p, s ("secret" word: apples)

Make: as, sap/spa, pal/lap, ape/pea, sea, slap/pals, peas, lapse, apple, apples

Sort: –ea (pea, sea); –ap (sap, lap, slap); plural (pals, peas, apples)

Transfer: clap, tea, flea, fleas

Making Words Letters: e, e, i, d, g, l, n, s ("secret" word: seedling)

Make: is, in, see, end/den/Ned, lid, slid, sign/sing, slide, sling, seeing, seeding, seedling

Sort: –id (lid, slid); –ing (sing, sling); suffix –ing (seeing, seeding)

Transfer: skid, ring, fling, ringing

APPLES

GUESS THE COVERED WORD

Write the sentences below on an overhead transparency or piece of chart paper. (Write the name of a student on each line. This makes the activity even more fun!) Cover the bold word in each sentence with two, dark colored self-stick notes—one note to cover the "onset" (all of the consonants before the first vowel) and the other note to cover the "rime" (the rest of the word). Let students have four guesses and write these guesses on the transparency or chart paper. Then, uncover the onset. Let students guess again, if necessary. Students will use context clues, beginning letters (onsets), and word length to guess the covered words in these sentences.

There are many ways to enjoy apples.

1. _____ likes apple **pies**.

2. _____ likes apple **cider**.

3. _____ likes apple **jelly**.

4. _____ likes apple **butter**.

5. _____ likes apple **tarts**.

WRITING

This is a mini-lesson you can write on a large piece of chart paper or an overhead transparency. The lesson is about things (facts) students have learned about apples. The purpose of this lesson is to model for the entire class how to write an informational piece.

As you write, share some things you know about apples and writing. Talk about how you begin each sentence with a capital letter and end each sentence with a period. Talk about what you are going to write about apples and why you are writing. This is what a finished piece might look like in a second- or third-grade class:

You can grow apple trees from seeds, but most orchards use cuttings. In 10 years, the planted tree is big enough to grow fruit. First, the tree is pruned to cut away dead branches. In the spring, apple trees have blossoms. That's when the apples will begin to grow. It will take 10 to 20 weeks for apples to ripen. In the fall, apples are picked, or harvested. People use the apples to make apple cider, apple juice, apple pies, and applesauce. Apples are a popular and tasty fruit.

In first grade, it might be even simpler. The idea is to write something similar to what many children in the class can write.

You can grow apple trees from seeds.

In the spring, apple trees have blossoms.

In the summer, apples ripen.

In the fall, apples are picked.

Students can choose to write about apples, apple trees, Johnny Appleseed, or anything they have learned while studying the apple theme.

ART ACTIVITIES

APPLE PAINTING

Bring in five or six varieties of apples—Granny Smith (green), Golden Delicious (yellow), Red Delicious (red), McIntosh (reddish), Stayman (red), etc.—so that you will have several sizes, shapes, and colors. Talk about the sizes, shapes, and colors of the apples. Show students how you would outline, and then fill in a painting of one of the apples. Then, give students large pieces of construction paper and red, yellow, or green paint. (It is their choice!) Let students paint large apples on their construction paper.

APPLE STAMPS

Cut several apples in half and carve a shape on each half. Let students dip the carved halves in paint and create their own apple stamp prints.

APPLES

FOOD ACTIVITY

APPLESAUCE

This recipe will make about eight cups of applesauce.

INGREDIENTS

- 8 apples
- 2 cups water
- ½ tsp. cinnamon (optional)
- ½ cup sugar (optional)

Caution: Before completing any food activity, ask families' permission and inquire about students' food allergies and religious or other food preferences.

DIRECTIONS

1. You, or a parent volunteer, should peel and core eight apples. Cut the apples into small pieces so that they will cook quickly.

2. Put the apple pieces in a medium pot with two cups of water. Cook the apples over medium-high heat until they are very soft. When the apples are finished cooking, add the cinnamon and sugar, if you wish.

3. Let the apples cool, then have children mash them into applesauce with a fork or a potato masher. Spoon the applesauce into an airtight container and store in the refrigerator until snack time, lunchtime, or the final celebration.

© CARSON-DELLOSA • INTEGRATING READING, WRITING, AND WORDS LESSONS • CD-104194

CULMINATING ACTIVITY

APPLE FESTIVAL

Have an apple festival in the classroom!

- **Bobbing for Apples:** Fill a plastic tub halfway with water and add 20 apples. Students should kneel in front of the tub, place their hands behind their backs, and try to capture the floating apples using just their mouths.

- **Story Time:** Read an apple book to students while they eat apples, applesauce, or individual apple pies.

- **Apple Sprouts:** Help students plant apple seeds that they removed from real apples so that the class can observe the growing process. Learning about apples is fun!

BEACH

Some children live near a beach or travel to a beach regularly. These children know what a beach is like and what happens when people visit a beach. Some children live far from the coastlines of their countries and don't have opportunities to visit ocean beaches. These children may visit lakes or rivers instead. Some children don't have opportunities to travel far from home, so they will learn a lot and have some fun as they read, write, and study about the beach.

SELF-SELECTED READING

Books for teachers to read aloud and then put in book baskets or on shelves for Self-Selected Reading:

FICTION

Out of the Ocean by Debra Frasier (Voyager Books, 2002)
As a mother and daughter walk along the beach, they enjoy the treasures cast up by the sea—feathers, shells, and even a bottle.

Young Cam Jansen and the Double Beach Mystery by David A. Adler (Puffin Books, 2003)
Girl sleuth Cam Jansen solves two seaside mysteries using her photographic memory. She successfully locates her mother after a walk and solves the case of the missing papers.

Curious George Goes to the Beach
(Houghton Mifflin Company, 1999)
Curious George visits the beach. He enjoys feeding the seagulls, saves a picnic basket from floating out to sea, and helps his friend stop being afraid of water.

How Will We Get to the Beach? by Brigitte Luciani (North-South Books, 2000)
One summer day, Roxanne prepares to go to the beach by loading up the car with her turtle, the umbrella, a book of wonderful stories, a ball, and her baby. When she finds that the car won't start, Roxanne decides to take the bus to the beach. But, something she wants to take can't go on the bus, so she tries several other modes of transportation. Each time, Roxanne discovers she must leave something behind. Finally, she perseveres. Students will have great fun guessing what can't go each time.

When the Tide Is Low by Sheila Cole (Lothrop, Lee, and Shepard Books, 1985)
A little girl and her mother talk about what they will do when the tide is low, and they walk on the beach. Her mother explains the tides by comparing them to her daughter's swinging.

BEACH

NONFICTION OR INFORMATIONAL BOOKS

On My Beach There Are Many Pebbles by Leo Lionni (HarperTrophy, 1994)
Beautiful black-and-white illustrations show beach pebbles in many different shapes: "fish pebbles," "people pebbles," "letter pebbles," and more.

All You Need for the Beach by Alice Schertle (Silver Whistle, 2004)
Using rhyming text, this book lists things that are essential for a fun time at the beach, such as a grain of sand, a beach umbrella, a bucket and shovel, and waves rolling that will tickle your toes.

On the Way to the Beach by Henry Cole (Greenwillow Books, 2003)
Readers are led on a nature walk through a marsh, dunes, and finally, the beach. Cole describes intriguing animals and plants along the way.

GUIDED READING

Choose a book about the beach that is just right for most children's reading levels. There are many books about the beach for grade two in most basal series. One book that works well for this activity is *A Salmon for Simon* by Betty Waterton and Ann Blades (Groundwood Books, 1998). This book can be found in most school libraries, on Guided Reading carts, or in book closets in schools that have gathered student texts for teachers to use.

BEFORE READING

Have students go on a scavenger hunt in the classroom and find a shovel, bucket, shell, fishing pole, towel, and beach ball you have previously hidden. Have students discuss **how** each item is used and guess **where** they might use the item.

Introduce the following vocabulary using the Rivet method (Cunningham, Hall, and Cunningham, 2000). Vocabulary words to introduce:

- coast
- channel
- clam digging
- tide
- strainer
- talons
- jellyfish
- salmon
- stream
- seagull

RIVET

Rivet is an activity created by Pat Cunningham one day while she was sitting in the back of a classroom watching a student teacher try to introduce some vocabulary words to her students. The vocabulary was important to the story, and many students needed to focus on the words and their meanings. The student teacher was diligently writing the words on the board and having students use them in sentences. She was also trying to help students access meanings and find relationships among the words. Unfortunately, the students were not particularly interested in the words, and their attention was marginal at best. After the student teacher had introduced the words and students began to read the selection, many of

the struggling readers couldn't decode the new words, much less associate meaning with them. Rivet was conceived that day and has since saved many teachers from the dreaded experience of teaching words that students don't seem to understand!

Activating students' prior knowledge and getting them to make predictions before they read is one way to increase the involvement and comprehension of most students. To prepare for a Rivet exercise, read the selection and pick 6–10 important words with a particular emphasis on big words. Include names of characters if they are interesting or difficult to decode. An important two-word phrase can also be included.

Begin the activity by drawing lines on the board to indicate how many letters each word has. (Some teachers have students draw the same number of lines on pieces of scratch paper and fill in letters as they are filled in on the board.)

Then, fill in the letters for the first word, one at a time, as students watch. Stop after each letter and see if anyone can guess the word. Students are not guessing letters; they are trying to guess each word as soon as they think they know what it is.

RIVET STEP-BY-STEP

1. Choose 6–10 important words in the text, including important names and words likely to be difficult to decode.

- coast
- channel
- clam digging
- tide
- strainer

- talons
- jellyfish
- salmon
- stream
- seagull

2. Draw lines on the board or an overhead transparency to indicate the number of letters in each word.

— — — — —

— — — — — — —

— — — —   — — — — — —

— — — —

— — — — — — —

— — — — — —

— — — — — — — —

— — — — — —

— — — — — —

— — — — — —

3. Fill in the blanks with the letters for each word, pausing after you write each letter to encourage students to guess the word. If someone guesses the word, finish writing it. (Unlike the game Hangman, students are not guessing letters. Their eyes are "riveted" to the board as you write letters, and they try to guess each word based on the letters you have written and the number of remaining blanks.)

c o a s t

c h a n n e l

c l a m   d i g g i n g

t i d e

s t r _ _ _ _ _

_ _ _ _ _ _

_ _ _ _ _ _ _ _

_ _ _ _ _ _

_ _ _ _ _ _

_ _ _ _ _ _

4. When you have written all of the words, have students use as many of the words as possible to make predictions about what is going to happen in the story. Record these predictions.

5. Have students read to determine which of their predictions were correct.

DURING READING
(PARTNER READING)

Tell students they are going to read a story about a little boy who goes fishing at the beach. They will read with partners to find out what happens in the story and how the boy solves a problem. Partners will take turns reading one page at a time.

AFTER READING

Use a permanent marker to write the following questions on an inflated beach ball:

- Who are the characters?

- Where and when did the story take place?

- What is the problem?

- How was it solved?

- What is the plot?

- Can you tell about another story you have read or an event that has happened in your life that was similar to this story?

Begin by asking students what problem the boy had at the beach. Then, toss the Beach Ball around for the children to catch and answer questions about the story. If the ball is tossed to a child, she must answer the question that her right thumb is touching when she catches the ball.

Tell students that when they read the story about a boy who went fishing at the beach, they learned how he solved his problem. Let them know that tomorrow, they will reread the story and talk about their favorite parts.

BEACH

WORKING WITH WORDS

MAKING WORDS

In these lessons, you dictate words, and students use small letter cards (or cut apart letter strips) to make these words. (The "secret" word is the last word made and uses all of the letters.) Next, lead students to sort the words for beginning sounds or spelling patterns. The final step is the transfer step. Have students use the sort patterns to decode and spell new words.

Making Words Letters: a, o, u, b, d, f, r, r, s, s ("secret" word: surfboards)

Make: as, ad, sad, bad, fad, for, our, oar, soar, sour, fuss, road, roads, board, boards, surfboards

Sort: –ad (ad, sad, bad, fad); –our (our, sour); –oar (oar, soar); plurals (roads, boards, surfboards)

Transfer: glad, scour, oars, pads

Making Words Letters: a, i, f, h, r, s, s, t ("secret" word: starfish)

Make: if, is, it, at, fat, sat, rat, hat, has, hats, rats, star, stars, stair, starfish

Sort: –at (at, fat, sat, rat, hat); plurals (hats, rats, stars)

Transfer: scat, flats, stairs

GUESS THE COVERED WORD

Write the sentences below on an overhead transparency or piece of chart paper. Cover the bold word in each sentence with two, dark colored self-stick notes—one note to cover the "onset" (all of the consonants before the first vowel) and the other note to cover the "rime" (the rest of the word). Let students have four guesses and write these guesses on the transparency or chart paper. Then, uncover the onset. Let students guess again, if necessary. Students will use context clues, beginning letters (onsets), and word length to guess the covered words in these sentences.

AT THE OCEAN

1. Jennifer **splashed** in the ocean.

2. We **walked** in the sand at the seashore.

3. I found **many** seashells for my collection.

4. Dad protected himself from the sun by putting on **lotion**.

5. My family's favorite beach activity is **swimming**.

BEACH

WRITING

Students often become overwhelmed when trying to write stories about entire events. Although they have great ideas and can verbally give you minute-by-minute accounts of activities, they have trouble putting their ideas on paper. This three-day activity involves thinking your thoughts out loud while writing them on a piece of chart paper. Each day, students will get to see you write one stage of a story (beginning, middle, or end). When presented with the concepts of beginning, middle, and end in this manner, children are better able to visualize and write longer, more focused, and detailed stories. Here are three mini-lessons a second- or third-grade teacher could write about a trip (real or imaginary) to the beach when she was a child. (For first graders, make it simple, like something a first grader could write.)

DAY 1
BEGINNING

One summer, I went to the beach with my family. It was a very long and very boring drive. I could not wait to get there! The first thing I did once my daddy parked the car was to run down to the sand and do cartwheels. Then, I put my feet in the cold, refreshing water. Later that afternoon, my mom and I went walking where the ocean meets the sand. We found several beautiful and unusual shells. I was looking down, and something white and round caught my eye. I started screaming because I was so excited. I had found a sand dollar!

DAY 2
MIDDLE

The next day was just as exciting. My dad took me fishing with him. We used a net to catch minnows. Then, we put them in my sand bucket. I loved watching them swim around in circles. When my dad wasn't looking, I let a few of them back into the ocean because I felt sorry for them. Dad would reach into the bucket, pick out a minnow, and put it on the hook for me. Then, he would let me cast the fishing line off the wooden pier. We waited and watched as my orange bobber rode the waves. It bobbed up and down as we waited for it to sink. When it finally sank, I reeled in my fishing line. Finally, Dad took over for me and pulled in a small fish that wiggled on the hook as he held it for me to see. After Dad took it off the hook, we threw it back. In fact, we threw back all of the fish we caught.

DAY 3
END

The last day at the beach, I decided to stay on the beach all day and build sand castles. I used wet sand and sticks to make a castle fit for a princess. When people walked by, they would tell me how beautiful it was. After several hours, the tide started coming in. Each time the waves crashed, they would steal part of my castle. My dad told me to get my sand toys and go back to the room to pack up; it was time to drive back to the city.

Even though I knew I would miss the sand, water, and warm sun, I was ready to go home. I couldn't wait to tell my friends about my vacation. It was the best time I ever had at the beach, and I will never forget it!

QUICK WRITES OR OTHER IDEAS FOR WRITING MINI-LESSONS

Here are a few Quick Writes that can be posted in the room so that children will have writing activities to work on. These ideas also could be used for other mini-lessons while learning about the beach.

- Describe a seashell you saw or found at the beach.

- What would you do if you found a message in a bottle? What would it say? What would you write back?

- Describe what you would see if you were standing on the beach.

- What are some activities that you can do on the beach?

- Write about a time you went to the beach. Make a list of the things you did while you were there.

BEACH

ART ACTIVITY

BEACH COLLAGE

MATERIALS

- Glue
- Play sand
- Seashells
- Blue and green tissue paper cut into ½" squares
- White construction paper
- Markers or crayons

DIRECTIONS

1. Have students place glue along the bottom of the paper (long edge). Then, let them sprinkle sand on the glue. Next, students should use glue to attach the blue and green tissue paper squares to look like water.

2. Students can decorate their collages with sand castles, shells, and ocean animals by drawing them or making them using glue, sand, and seashells.

CULMINATING ACTIVITY

BEACH DAY

Celebrate with a Beach Day!

- Let students wiggle their toes and play in a pile of play sand.

- Have students estimate the number of seashells in a bucket. Then, let them sort seashells into piles according to shape, size, or color.

- Have students bring beach towels, beach clothes (shorts, not swimsuits), sunglasses, and other beach items to school. Be sure you let them do the limbo.

- Let students go "fishing." Tie a 24" piece of yarn to the end of a ruler. Attach a magnet to the other end of the yarn. Cut several fish out of paper and attach paper clips to the fish's mouths. Write one of the following words on each fish—**beach**, **coast**, **towel**, **sand**, **shell**, or **kite**. Have students take turns using the magnetic fishing pole to catch "fish" and read the words.

  A student can keep a fish if he can say a word that rhymes with the word written on the fish.

BIKE RIDING

Do your students ride bikes? Many children who live in the suburbs have bikes to ride and places to ride them. Many city children, if they have bikes, learn how to ride them in nearby parks; it is in those same parks that they ride their bikes once they learn how. Farm and rural children sometimes have a hard time learning to ride their bicycles on gravel roads or paths. But, once farm children learn how to ride their bikes, they become quite good at navigating these gravel roads and paths. Getting over the fear of falling is usually the biggest hurdle for young children. But, children can become good at anything they work at, and all children seem to learn to ride! Bike riding is good exercise, as well as a good way to get from one place to another.

SELF-SELECTED READING

Books for teachers to read aloud and then put in book baskets or on shelves for Self-Selected Reading:

FICTION

Duck on a Bike by David Shannon (Blue Sky Press, 2002)
Duck takes a wild journey around the farm on a red bike and gets many different reactions from his fellow farm animals.

The Bike Lesson by Jan and Stan Berenstain (Random House Books for Young Readers, 1964)
As Papa Bear tries to show Brother Bear how to ride his new bike, young readers will love to see that Papa Bear is the one who really needs the lessons.

Bear on a Bike by Stella Blackstone (Barefoot Books, 2001)
A bear takes a boy on a fun romp using various methods of transportation, including riding a bike.

Franklin Rides a Bike by Paulette Bourgeois (Scholastic Paperbacks, 1997)
After watching his friends learn to ride without their training wheels, Franklin is determined to join their two-wheeled adventures.

Gus and Grandpa and the Two-Wheeled Bike by Claudia Mills (Farrar, Straus and Giroux, 2001)
With the help of an old bike, Gus's grandpa gently guides him through the scary experience of learning to ride without training wheels.

Big Bird's Big Bike by Anna Ross (Random House Books for Young Readers, 1993) With some help from his monster pal Grover, Big Bird learns to ride a bicycle.

Mike and the Bike by Michael Ward (Cookie Jar Publishing, 2005) Mike celebrates the joy of having a bike as he pedals his way around the world. Includes a CD with kid-friendly songs.

Poppleton in Spring by Cynthia Rylant (Blue Sky Press, 1999) Poppleton the pig returns in some new springtime adventures. He cleans, sleeps in a tent, and faces many choices while shopping for a bike.

The Mystery of the Stolen Bike by Marc Brown (Little, Brown and Company, 1998) Arthur's friend Francine is not proud of having a hand-me-down bike, but she misses it when it is stolen.

Julian's Glorious Summer by Ann Cameron (Rebound by Sagebrush, 1999) In this easy chapter book, Julian's friend Gloria has a new bike. Julian tells a fib to cover his fear of bikes, but eventually, he learns that bikes are fun.

NONFICTION OR INFORMATIONAL BOOKS

I Can Ride a Bike by Edana Eckart (Children's Press, 2002) A boy named Tim goes for a bike ride with his mom. Photographs depict Tim riding and correctly using safety equipment. A glossary is included at the end of the book.

The Bicycle Man by Allen Say (Houghton Mifflin Company, 1989) Set in Japan, this book shows how having fun on a bike overcomes cultural differences.

GUIDED READING

Franklin Rides a Bike by Paulette Bourgeois (Scholastic Paperbacks, 1997) will work for first, second, and third grades. In some first-grade classes, this book can be read at the end of the year. In this case, as well as in second grade, this story can be divided into two parts. However, in third grade, students will often be able to read and make "text-to-self" connections in one day.

DAY 1
BEFORE READING

Talk about text-to-self connections and tell students how you learned to ride a bicycle and how you felt when you first got on one. Remind students to think about these text-to-self connections as they read the first half of the book. Then, use the Rivet strategy (page 26) to introduce the following vocabulary:

- training wheels
- practiced
- worried
- explorers
- groaned
- guided
- pedaling
- frustrating
- padding

DURING READING (PARTNER READING)

Have students read with partners; partners will take turns reading one page at a time. They will read the first half of the book, or approximately eight pages, so each student will read four pages. (There are about 16 pages

of text and as many pages of pictures.) Next, tell students to talk about any text-to-self connections they had when reading the first half of the story. To help with text-to-self connections, have students think of answers to these questions, "Have you ever felt like Franklin? Do you have friends who learned to ride their bicycles without training wheels before you learned? How did that make you feel?"

AFTER READING

Give students a few minutes to share their text-to-self connections with their partners. Then, let some students share their connections with the class. Make a list on a piece of chart paper or an overhead transparency of students' text-to-self connections from the first half of the book.

DAY 2

BEFORE READING

Review the story so far and talk about some text-to-self connections from yesterday. Tell students they will finish reading the book today and ask them to look for more text-to-self connections in the second half of the book. Ask students to think about these questions, "How did you learn to ride your bike? Who helped you learn to ride? How did that person help? How did you feel when you were learning?"

DURING READING (SAME PARTNERS)

Have students finish reading the book with their partners, taking turns and making text-to-self connections.

AFTER READING

Give students five minutes to share their connections with their partners. Next, have students share their connections with the entire class. Then, talk about the ending, students' connections, and how their connections helped them understand the story.

WORKING WITH WORDS

MAKING WORDS

In these lessons, you dictate words, and students use small letter cards (or cut apart letter strips) to make these words. (The "secret" word is the last word made and uses all of the letters.) Next, lead students to sort the words for beginning sounds or spelling patterns. The final step is the transfer step. Have students use the sort patterns to decode and spell new words.

Making Words Letters: i, g, h, l, s, t ("secret" word: lights)

Make: is, it, hit, sit/its, his, hits/this, list/slit, sigh, sight, light, slight, lights

Sort: sl– (slit, slight); –it (it, hit, sit, slit); –ight (sight, light, slight)

Transfer: fit, skit, might, bright

Making Words Letters: a, e, i, c, c, p, r, t ("secret" word: practice)

Make: at, it, pit, pat, rat/art, car, act, ice, rice, ripe, part, price, pirate, carpet, practice

Sort: –it (it, pit); –at (at, pat, rat); –ice (ice, rice, price, practice)

Transfer: fit, brat, slice, twice

GUESS THE COVERED WORD

Write the sentences below on an overhead transparency or piece of chart paper. Cover the bold word in each sentence with two, dark colored self-stick notes—one note to cover the "onset" (all of the consonants before the first vowel) and the other note to cover the "rime" (the rest of the word). Let students have four guesses and write these guesses on the transparency or chart paper. Then, uncover the onset. Let students guess again, if necessary. Students will use context clues, beginning letters (onsets), and word length to guess the covered words in these sentences.

1. It is fun riding a **blue** bike.

2. Bicycles have two **pedals**.

3. I have fun riding with my **friend**.

4. My **mother** taught me how to ride.

5. To be safe, I wear a **helmet**.

WRITING

For students in grades two and three, writing personal narratives about learning to ride a bike or times when they went bike riding are appropriate and often amusing. Students like mini-lessons in which their teachers write personal narratives about learning to ride a bike. When writing for your mini-lesson, remind students that the beginning paragraph needs to tell who, what, where, when, and why. The middle paragraph elaborates on the problem. The final paragraph solves the problem or tells how the story ends.

I (who) remember when I learned to ride a bike (what). I was seven years old (when), and my friend Beverly got a red bike for her birthday. I went down the block to her house (where), and we both tried to ride her bike. We tried and tried to ride her new big two-wheeler without wobbling. Her dad helped us by running behind us to keep us upright and heading in the right direction (how). We both learned to ride because riding is good exercise and lots of fun (why). Months later, when I got my own bike, we would go riding off together on our bikes.

BIKE RIDING

QUICK WRITES OR OTHER IDEAS FOR WRITING MINI-LESSONS

Here are a few Quick Writes that can be posted in the room so that children will have writing activities to work on. These ideas also could be used for other mini-lessons while learning about bike riding.

- Describe how you would teach someone to ride a bike.

- Write about your very first bike.

- Finish this sentence: If I had a bike I would . . . .

- Write a story about a big bike race.

- Describe your favorite places to ride a bike.

ART ACTIVITY

BICYCLE PORTRAITS

Have each student draw a picture of someone riding a bike or a picture of a bike she would like to have. Provide pictures of bicycles and helmets (catalog photos work well) for students who do not have bikes of their own as reference.

FOOD ACTIVITY

BIKING SNACKS

Make trail mix for a biking snack and serve with cold, bottled water.

Caution: Before completing any food activity, ask families' permission and inquire about students' food allergies and religious or other food preferences.

Send notes to several parents who often can't come to school to help but are happy to provide materials for projects or snacks. Recruit four parents to provide one six-pack of bottled water each. Ask six other parents to provide the ingredients for the trail mix: one 20-ounce box of square rice cereal, one 20-ounce box of square wheat cereal, one 15-ounce box of raisins, one 16-ounce can of peanuts, one 6-ounce bag of dried cranberries, and one 6-ounce bag of dried apples (or other bite-sized dried fruit that most children like). You can include one 21-ounce bag of candy-covered chocolates if you wish. Ask parents to bring their items to school a few days before you need them. (In case someone forgets, he can then send it the next day.) You might need to be the "backup buyer," but hopefully, you won't be responsible for buying everything. Some schools also have PTA or class funds for special projects like this. If your school does not, then check with your PTA, principal, or local organizations with volunteer time or money to help local causes. There are even Internet sources that fund these types of projects.

BIKE RIDING

TRAIL MIX

INGREDIENTS

- 20-ounce box of square rice cereal

- 20-ounce box of square wheat cereal

- 15-ounce box of raisins

- 16-ounce can of peanuts

- 6-ounce bag of dried cranberries

- 6-ounce bag of dried apples (or other bite-sized dried fruit that most children like)

- 21-ounce bag of candy-coated chocolates (optional)

DIRECTIONS

1. In a large mixing bowl, add the cereal, raisins, peanuts, cranberries, apples (or other dried fruit), and perhaps a bag of colorful, candy-coated chocolates if the weather is not too hot. (Be sure no students are allergic to peanuts or any of the other ingredients. If students are allergic, make a separate mix without that ingredient.)

2. Stir the ingredients together. Scoop the trail mix into small paper cups and serve with cold bottles of water.

CULMINATING ACTIVITY

BIKE RODEO

- Have bike safety lessons or organize bike races on the playground. Serve the trail mix and water when there is a break in the action.

- Watch a video of a bike race, such as the Tour de France. Serve the trial mix and water while students watch the riders pedal.

CAMPING

Camping can be a wonderful adventure for children. It exposes them to the simplicity of nature—no phones, no TV, and no computers. Camping increases a person's awareness of her surroundings and can refresh her appreciation for the many things that often go unnoticed. There are so many amazing things to discover in a natural setting—birds, animals, plants, trees, rocks, streams, ponds, insects, sounds, weather, and wildflowers. There are also many activities that provide fun and excitement for campers. Getting children interested in camping and nature while they are young can set them on a path to a lifetime of outdoor adventures.

SELF-SELECTED READING

Books for teachers to read aloud and then put in book baskets or on shelves for Self-Selected Reading:

FICTION

When We Go Camping by Margreit Ruurs (Tundra Books, 2001)
Beautiful, realistic paintings highlight all of the fabulous experiences to be found on a camping trip. The family raises the cooler to keep it from bears, identifies berries to eat, canoes down a river, and finds an abundance of wildlife (elk, raccoons, and birds), many of which are discussed in the back of the book.

Camping Out by Mercer Mayer (School Specialty Publishing, 2001)
Little Critter and Gator camp out in the backyard. Strange noises turn out to be harmless—especially the crunching sound of a plate of cookies.

Amelia Bedelia Goes Camping by Peggy Parish (HarperTrophy, 2003)
Conscientious maid Amelia Bedelia precisely follows typical camping trip instructions, such as pitching a tent and rowing boats.

Bailey Goes Camping by Kevin Henkes (HarperTrophy, 1997)
Since Bailey is too young to go camping with his brother and sister who are Bunny Scouts, his parents let him do all of the fun activities at home.

The Berenstain Bears Go to Camp by Jan and Stan Berenstain (Random House Books for Young Readers, 1982)
The Berenstain brother and sister go to camp for the first time and learn that camp is fun—even when it means sleeping outside and having a powwow.

© CARSON-DELLOSA • INTEGRATING READING, WRITING, AND WORDS LESSONS • CD-104194

Arthur Goes to Camp by Marc Brown
(Little, Brown and Company, 1984)
After getting poison ivy and losing to girls in sports, Arthur plans to run away from camp but changes his mind as he inadvertently wins the scavenger hunt for his team.

Monk Camps Out by Emily Arnold McCully
(Arthur A. Levine Books, 2000)
Monk the mouse is embarking on his first backyard campout—by himself. He and his doting parents somehow manage to make it through the night.

Where the River Begins by Thomas Locker
(Puffin Books, 1993)
In this gloriously illustrated book, a grandfather takes his two grandsons on a camping trip to find the source of the river that passes by their home.

P. J. Funnybunny Camps Out by
Marilyn Sadler (Random House Books for Young Readers, 1994)
P. J. and his friends insist that "camping is not for girls." The clever girls decide to show them that camping can be challenging for boys, too.

NONFICTION OR INFORMATIONAL BOOKS

Camping by Tim Seeberg (Child's World, 2004)
Seeberg covers the basics of camping: different types of camping, ways to plan a camping trip, what equipment to bring, how to be safe, and more.

I Can Go Camping by Edana Eckart
(Children's Press, 2003)
Simple, easy-to-read text tells about a boy who goes camping with his family. He describes the fun experiences of setting up camp, cooking over a fire, and sleeping in a tent.

Park Rangers by Mary Firestone
(Bridgestone Books, 2003)
Part of a community helpers series, this book introduces the responsibilities of park rangers in both state and national parks. Topics, such as uniforms, vehicles, and training, are all addressed.

Wildfire! by Annie Auerbach (Little Simon, 2004)
This book looks at the heroic firefighters and smoke jumpers who work around the clock to contain dangerous forest and wilderness fires. Readers will learn about the equipment, techniques, and chemicals used to contain these destructive fires.

CAMPING

GUIDED READING

Choose a book for the whole class to read and enjoy. *Henry and Mudge and the Starry Night* by Cynthia Rylant (Aladdin, 1999) is a book that first graders can read at the end of the year (a good time to talk about camping), and second and third graders can read and enjoy independently.

DAY 1
BEFORE READING

Talk about times you or students in your class have gone camping. These are text-to-self connections. Set up a campsite in an area of your classroom. Include a tent, "campfire," lantern, and backpack. Teach students campfire songs. You can also have students sit around the campfire and play "Campfire Telephone." To play, one person starts by squeezing the person's hand to his right. This can be a soft squeeze followed by a hard squeeze or a series of squeezes. The students continue around the circle until the squeeze message gets back to the person who started it. Talk about how much the "message" changed. Let students take turns going inside the tent. Go on a "hike" around the school. Have students wear their backpacks. You can also have students brainstorm what they would take on a camping trip.

VOCABULARY

Introduce the following vocabulary:

- backpack
- campfire
- lantern
- tent
- waterfall
- shivered
- snuggled

Scramble each word and have students see if they can guess the word and use it in a sentence. For example, *kpacbcak* is backpack.

DURING READING (ERT)

Tell students, "Today we are going to read a story about a family that goes camping and hiking." Have students read the story using the ERT method (Cunningham, Hall, and Cunningham, 2000) described below.

EVERYONE READ TO . . .

"Everyone Read To . . ." or ERT is a during-reading format that teachers can use to guide children through the text, one or two pages at a time. Teachers use ERT when they want students to do the initial reading on their own, and they want to help students understand the important information on each page. This format can be used with small groups or the whole class. Even children who struggle with reading can often read better if they have a specific **purpose** for reading. Their success motivates them to continue to try.

When using ERT, first tell students how much to read. After they read that segment, follow up on the purpose you set by asking questions like: "What is the author telling us? What new things did you learn? What seems to be the problem in the story?" In their own words, students answer the questions based on what they read. Then, everyone goes to the next segment.

For older students, ERT is usually silent reading. However, because children must develop some reading fluency before they can

"read in their minds," ERT time with young children is usually not silent but is called "whisper" reading.

For ERT, choose a text that will require page-by-page guidance. Have students read the text by themselves to find or figure out the specific information they will share with the class. Plan before- and after-reading activities that will develop comprehension strategies.

ERT STEP-BY-STEP

1. Lead students through the text one or two pages at a time. Have students read about important events or information.

2. Have students read for purposes that are not literally stated but can be inferred. For example, you might say, "Read to find out how Charlie is feeling." The text may say it has been a bad day, and Charlie is stomping down the street. Students have to infer Charlie's feelings and explain how they know.

3. Have students raise their hands when they read a part where they find or figure out the information and then continue reading. Warn students when you set two purposes or there are two answers: These are "two-handers" because each student raises two hands. (Students love this!)

4. When most hands are up, ask a volunteer to give you the information. Ask another student to read the text aloud that helped him find or figure out the answers.

5. When the information is not literally stated, ask children to explain how they figured it out. You might say, "Yes, he is feeling bad and unhappy. It didn't say that in the text, but you figured it out. What did it say that helped you figure it out?"

Below is a series of ERT purposes for *Henry and Mudge and the Starry Night*:

- "Everyone read the first three pages to find out what Henry's mom and dad know about camping."

- "Everybody read the next two pages to find out what animals Henry thinks they will see."

- "Everybody read the next page to find out what each family member, even Mudge, takes along on the camping trip."

- "Everybody read the next two pages to find out what Henry sees on the hike."

- "Everyone read the next two pages to find out what Mudge smells on the hike."

- "Everyone read the next page to find out what they unpack at the campsite."

- "Everybody read the next page to find out how Henry and Mudge feel about the one thing they need to make the camp ready."

- "Everyone read the next two pages to find out what they do before falling asleep. This is a two-hander."

- "Everyone read the next two pages to see how the family feels about sleeping under the stars."

- "Everybody read the last page to find out how well everyone sleeps."

AFTER READING

Assign partners and have them retell the important events in the story to each other. Then, choose one or two students to share their retellings with the entire class.

DAY 2
BEFORE READING

Rereading is important for fluency. For Day Two, form Playschool Groups of five students. Give each group a set of index cards with the name of a character written on each card (Henry, Mudge, Mom, Dad, and Narrator). Give the Narrator card to the best reader in each group. Then, give individual character cards to the rest of the group.

DURING READING ("DOING THE BOOK")

Have students read the story together. The Narrator reads all of the text except what is in quotation marks. The individual characters read what their characters say in the story. When they are finished, ask each student to write a favorite quote from any character and be ready to read it to the class.

AFTER READING

Have students make a journal of Henry's camping trip. Construct small, three-page journals (5" x 7") with card stock covers. Then, let students write what happened at the beginning, middle, and end of the story and how Henry must have felt during those times. Finally, have students collect small sticks and glue them to their covers.

WORKING WITH WORDS

MAKING WORDS

In these lessons, you dictate words, and students use small letter cards (or cut apart letter strips) to make these words. (The "secret" word is the last word made and uses all of the letters.) Next, lead students to sort the words for beginning sounds or spelling patterns. The final step is the transfer step. Have students use the sort patterns to decode and spell new words.

Making Words Letters: a, e, i, c, f, m, p, r ("secret" word: campfire)

Make: am, Pam, ram, ace, ice, mice, rice, face, pace, race, came, fame, camp, ramp, price, frame, camper, fire, campfire

Sort: –am (am, Pam, ram); –ice (ice, mice, rice, price); –ace (ace, face, race); –ame (came, fame, frame); –amp (camp, ramp)

Transfer: scram, slice, space, game, stamp

Making Words Letters: a, a, o, h, l, l, m, m, r, s, s, w ("secret" word: marshmallows)

Make: am, ham, arm, mow, row, low, all, mall, hall, harm, small, slam, slow, alarm, marshmallows

Sort: –am (am, ham, slam); –ow (mow, row, low, slow); –all (all, mall, hall, small); –arm (arm, harm, alarm)

Transfer: scam, blow, stall, charm

CAMPING

Making Words Letters: a, e, l, n, n, r, t
("secret" word: lantern)

Make: Al, at, rat, an, ran, tan, let, net, eat/ate
ear, near, tear, rate, late, Nate, neat, teal/tale,
real, lane, rent, later, lantern

Sort: –an (an, ran, tan); –ate (ate, rate, late,
Nate); –eat (eat, neat); –eal (teal, real)

Transfer: pan, date, treat, steal

GUESS THE COVERED WORD

Write the passage below on an overhead transparency or piece of chart paper. Cover the bold word in each sentence with two, dark colored self-stick notes—one note to cover the "onset" (all of the consonants before the first vowel) and the other note to cover the "rime" (the rest of the word). Let students have four guesses and write these guesses on the transparency or chart paper. Then, uncover the onset. Let students guess again, if necessary. Students will use context clues, beginning letters (onsets), and word length to guess the covered words in these sentences.

TOMMY'S CAMPING TRIP

Tommy **helped** his father set up the tent. After that, his father built a campfire. They cooked **hamburgers** over the fire. After lunch they went for a **swim**. Tommy and his dad saw a **deer**. When it got dark, Tommy told his dad **scary** stories. Tommy was very **tired** when he got into his sleeping bag.

WRITING

Getting students to use more descriptive words in their writing can be an ongoing problem. A good way to show students the importance of descriptive words is to write a "plain" story for your mini-lesson on day one. On day two, have students help you make the story more interesting by adding more descriptive words to your "plain" story. Each time a student adds a better word or descriptive adjective to the plain story, you (or the student) use a caret (^) to mark the spot and write the more descriptive word or the adjective. Finding and adding descriptive words to your short story will help students as they look at their own work and make changes. After this warm-up exercise, have students write their own camping stories. Then, have them look at their stories with partners, to add more descriptive words.

CAMPING

DAY 1
A PLAIN STORY

One day, it was Austin's birthday. Dad decided to take us camping in the woods. There was one problem. We had heard there was a bear living in the woods. People called the bear Fangs because he had big teeth and growled when he was mad. I was scared!

Austin said he was too scared to go camping. Dad had already packed the car, so we were going. Once we got to the campground, Dad picked out a good place to camp. We helped Dad set up the tent and collect some wood. Later that day, we were ready to start the fire. We heard a sound coming from the woods, but Dad told us not to worry. We began cooking our hot dogs over the fire. We ate them, and then, we had s'mores and hot chocolate for dessert. After dinner, we were sleepy, so we went to bed. We fell asleep in minutes.

Later, Austin yelled as the bear came into our tent! The bear looked like he hadn't eaten in days. We threw him our hot dogs and s'mores. The bear ate and left. In the morning, we told Dad what happened, but he just said, "Yeah." The next time we go camping, we will make sure we pack lots of food in case we meet another bear!

DAY 2
MAKING IT BETTER

One day, it was Austin's ^seventh^ birthday. Dad decided to take us camping in the woods. There was one problem. We had heard there was ^wild^ a bear living in the woods. People called the bear Fangs because he had ~~big~~ ^enormous^ teeth and growled when he was mad. I was scared!

Austin said he was too scared to go camping. Dad had already packed the ^station wagon^ ~~car~~, so we were going. Once we got to the campground, Dad picked out a ^safe^ ~~good~~ place to camp. We helped Dad set up the tent and collect some ~~wood~~ ^firewood^. Later that day, we were ready to start the fire. We heard a ^strange^ sound coming from ^deep in^ the woods, but Dad told us not to worry. We began cooking our hot dogs over the fire. We ate them, and then, we had s'mores and hot chocolate for dessert. After dinner, we were sleepy, so we ^got into our sleeping bags^ ~~went to bed~~. We fell asleep in minutes.

Later, Austin ~~yelled~~ ^screamed^ as the bear came into our tent! The bear looked like he hadn't eaten in ^a few^ days. We threw him our ^leftover^ hot dogs and s'mores. The bear ate ^quickly^ and left. In the morning, we told Dad what happened, but he just said, "Yeah." The next time we go camping, we will make sure we pack lots of ^extra^ food in case we meet another ^hungry^ bear!

45

PERSONAL NARRATIVE

Writing personal narratives can be the easiest form of writing for most primary students. However, the ease of using this style depends on the number of experiences a student has had with the topic. When young children do not have experiences to write from, you have two options: create the experiences for them or give them another topic. It may be better to share books and other stories with children. These experiences allow each student to come up with enough ideas to write a personal narrative of his own. Maybe he never went camping in a tent, but he spent a night in his grandparents' RV. Students can make these connections as they build more background knowledge about a topic you are asking them to write about. Below is a sample from a mini-lesson on personal narrative you can share with your class. First, write the story. Then, have students identify the sentences with details. (These sentences are underlined in the sample.) After students identify each detail sentence, talk about how the sentence tells the audience a little bit more about the topic.

My grandfather took me camping during spring break this year. We went to the tallest mountain in North Carolina. When we got to the mountain, we looked for a flat spot. We wanted to make sure we had a nice place to put up the tent. After we set up the tent, we built a small fire. We put hot dogs on the ends of sticks and cooked them over the fire. After lunch, we went for a hike on the nature trail. While we were hiking, my Pop-Pop told me the name of every plant we saw. Finally, when it started to get dark, we hiked back to the campsite and ate dinner. We also sang songs around the campfire.

I was sad when it was time to go home. We had so much fun in the mountains. I hope Pop-Pop will take me again next spring.

QUICK WRITES OR OTHER IDEAS FOR WRITING MINI-LESSONS

Here are a few Quick Writes that can be posted in the room so that children will have writing activities to work on. These ideas also could be used for other mini-lessons while learning about camping.

- Write a make-believe story about running into a bear while you are hiking or camping in the woods.

- After you set up your campsite, you go fishing. Write about what you do when the fish you catch asks you to throw him back.

- Write about a time you went camping.

- Your family is planning a camping trip. Write about what you are going to pack.

CAMPING

ART ACTIVITY

FIREFLIES IN A JAR

MATERIALS

- Black construction paper
- Wax paper
- Aluminum foil
- Glow-in-the-dark confetti or fluorescent paper
- Glue
- Tape
- Scissors
- Hole punch (optional)
- Pencils

DIRECTIONS

1. Provide each student glow-in-the-dark confetti or let him use a hole punch on fluorescent paper to create his own confetti. Give each student a piece of construction paper and have him glue the confetti randomly on one side of the paper. If you want to provide "fireflies" that are more realistic, you can often find small glow-in-the-dark insects at party supply stores.

2. Have each student roll his piece of paper into a cylinder with the confetti side out and tape it together. When the paper is rolled into a cylinder, it resembles a jar (just like the one your grandma used to give you).

3. Tell each student to cover his cylinder with a layer of wax paper and secure it with tape. (This will make it look like the fireflies are in a jar.) If needed, students should trim any excess wax paper.

4. Give each student a piece of aluminum foil and let him cut and shape it to fit over the top of the cylinder to make a "lid" for his "jar." Remind students to use a sharpened pencil to punch holes in the lids of their jars so that the fireflies can get air.

When you turn off the lights, each student will have a jar of his own "glowing fireflies," just as if he had gone camping and caught them.

CAMPING

FOOD ACTIVITY

INDOOR S'MORES

Nothing says camping like the word s'mores. Following is a recipe for making excellent Indoor S'mores.

Caution: Before completing any food activity, ask families' permission and inquire about students' food allergies and religious or other food preferences.

INGREDIENTS

- Chocolate bars
- Marshmallow cream
- Graham crackers

DIRECTIONS

1. Help each student break one whole graham cracker into four smaller crackers. Let each student spread one spoonful of marshmallow cream on each cracker piece.

2. Break the chocolate bars into squares and give each student two squares. Tell students to place the squares on top of the marshmallow cream on their crackers and cover them with the other cracker pieces to make sandwiches.

3. Let students enjoy their s'mores!

CULMINATING ACTIVITY

CLASSROOM CAMPING

- Invite students to wear camping clothes or pajamas and bring their sleeping bags. Set up an area in your classroom that represents a campsite. You can put up a sheet in a corner or bring in an actual tent. Make a "campfire" using rolled newspaper or paper towel tubes as "logs" and tissue paper as "fire."

- Gather students around the campfire and tell stories, sing songs, etc., while they eat the Indoor S'mores.

CITIES

Big cities can be exciting places. There are people walking here and there—to school, to stores, and to the subway. Taxis are hurrying to take people where they want to go. Traffic lights are changing, signs are shining, and horns are honking. There are workers making repairs and buildings being built. Restaurants and shops are found on almost every corner. People living high up in apartments and people staying in high-rise hotels are looking down on everything. There are many things going on in a city—so much to see and so much to do!

For children who live in rural areas, all of this information seems strange. Some children have never seen a skyscraper, a high-rise hotel, an elevator, a subway, an escalator, or busy city streets. For some children, life is quiet and slow paced, and they probably prefer it that way. If these children read a story about a subway or a taxi, they really don't fully understand it. Why? They have no background knowledge! Here are some ideas and activities for a Cities theme to help students who have never lived in or visited a city and provide vicarious experiences for students who lack their own experiences.

SELF-SELECTED READING

Books for teachers to read aloud and then put in book baskets or on shelves for Self-Selected Reading:

FICTION

Wheels on the Bus by Paul O. Zelinski (Orchard Books, 2002)
This story (and well-liked children's song) tells the adventures of a bus as it goes through a busy city.

Eloise by Kay Thompson (Simon & Schuster, 1969)
Read about an amazing little girl named Eloise who lives in grand style in the Plaza Hotel in New York City.

Richard Scarry's Busy, Busy Town by Richard Scarry (Golden Books, 2000)
This beginning reader introduces children to a busy town and all of the workers who make the town run.

Smoky Night by Eve Bunting (Voyager Books, 1999)
In this book inspired by true events, a young boy, his mother, and their neighbor weather the storm of an inner-city riot.

49

The Adventures of Taxi Dog by Debra and Sal Barracca (Dial, 1990)
When a taxi driver befriends Maxi the stray dog, the dog becomes a popular fixture on the driver's trips around the city.

Curious George Takes a Job by H. A. Rey (Houghton Mifflin Company, 1974)
Curious George escapes from the zoo and explores the metro, a bus, a restaurant, and a freshly-painted room in a skyscraper.

NONFICTION OR INFORMATIONAL BOOKS

Alphabet City by Stephen T. Johnson (Puffin, 1999)
In this wordless alphabet book, everyday objects, such as sawhorses, lamp posts, and park benches, are transformed into recognizable letters.

ABC NYC: A Book of Seeing New York City by Joanne Dugan (Harry N. Abrams, 2000)
This photographic introduction to New York teaches familiar city words—in alphabetical order, of course.

The Big Dig: Reshaping an American City by Peter Vanderwarker (Little, Brown and Company, 2001)
Explore the history of traffic problems in Boston, Massachusetts, and how technology has allowed a tunnel project to correct mistakes and rebuild neighborhoods in this busy city.

My Town at Work by Gare Thompson (National Geographic Society, 2002)
This book is about a town and its many public places and services that meet the needs of its citizens.

Our Town by Faridah Usof (National Geographic Society, 2001)
This book uses photographs to show how a town changes over time from a small hamlet with a few shops to a larger place with many shops and more schools.

A Good Place to Live by Marvin Buckley (National Geographic Society, 2001)
Photographs of all kinds of community helpers show how citizens benefit from the services of people who work for the common good.

Home by Jeannie Baker (Greenwillow Books, 2000)
As baby Tracy grows up watching out her window, she witnesses people improving her neighborhood and cleaning up her environment until her own child is born into a neighborhood that has been reborn.

Wow! City! by Robert Neubecker (Hyperion, 2004)
A toddler raised in the country visits a city and finds plenty of reasons to be wowed by it. Toddlers and older children alike will enjoy the artwork and join in with the "Wows!"

CITIES

GUIDED READING

Wheels on the Bus by Paul O. Zelinski (Orchard Books, 2002) is a book version of the well-liked children's song. It tells about the adventures of a bus as it goes through a busy city. There are other similar versions of the story available. Any of them can be used for this lesson, which is appropriate for first grade (early in the year) or as an easy lesson for second grade.

BEFORE READING

Take a "picture walk" through the book with your students. Talk about what is happening on each page. Ask students, "What do you think the story will be about?" (predicting). Talk about the people on the bus (characters), the city (setting), and what happened in the book (plot). Many students will accurately predict the whole story by taking a picture walk through the book.

DURING READING (ECHO READING)

Tell students that after they read the book, they are going to talk about what happened. They will put the actions in the order (sequence) that they read them. Echo read the book with students. Read the text aloud one page at a time and then have students become your echo, reading what you read.

AFTER READING

Talk about what happened in this story. Were students' predictions correct? If students have ever ridden on a city bus, let them share their experiences. Help students make text-to-self connections. Finally, make a list of everything that happened in this book (wheels go round, wipers go swish, horn goes beep, driver says "Move on back," people talk, babies cry, people say, "Shh," etc.). Help students put everything in the correct order or sequence. Reread the book chorally (students reading with you) to make sure

that they have correctly sequenced the events in the book.

CITY ALPHABET BOOK

At any grade level, read an alphabet book like *Alphabet City* by Stephen T. Johnson (Puffin, 1999) and make a class city-alphabet book. Instead of using just pictures like *Alphabet City*, use city words. Here are some examples:

- A—airport
- B—buses, bridges
- C—carts, cars, carriages
- D—doors
- E—elevators, escalators
- F—fire escapes
- G—girls, guys
- H—handles, hotels, hats
- I—ice cream shops
- J—juice, junk
- K—keys, kitchens, kites in the park
- L—lights, libraries
- M—men, movies, malls
- N—newspaper, newspaper stands
- O—oranges (on a fruit stand), orchestra
- P—pipes, pizza places, people
- R—rails, rushing, restaurants
- S—signs, subway, stoplights
- T—trees, tunnels
- U—umbrellas, underground openings
- V—vendors
- W—windows, women
- Y—yellow lights
- Z—zoo

Write a city alphabet list on a piece or two of chart paper. Then, choose a letter and model for students how they will complete their pages for the class alphabet book. First, write the letter on a large piece of construction paper. Next, write a city word that begins with that letter. Finally, draw a picture that illustrates the word. Each student will make one page.

After you model the process (letter, word, and drawing), have each student repeat the process. If there aren't enough students for all 26 letters, give the extra letters to students who finish the task quickly and do a good job. If you have more than 26 students, let the extra students work on the front cover, title page, table of contents, and back cover. Use a bookbinder, stapler, or large binder rings to assemble the book. You will have a class book to add to your Self-Selected Reading materials!

WORKING WITH WORDS

MAKING WORDS

In these lessons, you dictate words, and students use small letter cards (or cut apart letter strips) to make these words. (The "secret" word is the last word made and uses all of the letters.) Next, lead students to sort the words for beginning sounds or spelling patterns. The final step is the transfer step. Have students use the sort patterns to decode and spell new words.

Making Words Letters: a, a, e, m, n, p, r, t, t, s ("secret" word: apartments)

Make: me, ear, near, tear, team, ramp, area, arena, apart, spear, smear, stamp, tramp, steam, stream, patterns, apartments

Sort: –ear (ear, near, tear, spear, smear); –eam (team, steam, stream); –amp (ramp, stamp, tramp)

Transfer: fear, clear, gleam, clamp

Making Words Letters: e, i, b, d, g, r, s ("secret" word: bridges)

Make: Ed, red, bed, big, rig, dig, rid, ride, side, bird, bride, ridge, bridge, bridges

Sort: –ed (Ed, red, bed); –ig (big, rig, dig); –ide (ride, side, bride); –idge (ridge, bridge)

Transfer: sled, twig, slide, fridge

Making Words Letters: a, o, c, k, l, r, s, s, s, w ("secret" word: crosswalks)

Make: as, saw, law, claw, slaw, slow, crow, sock, lock, rock, rack, sack, walk, cross, Carol, across, crosswalks

Sort: –aw (saw, law, claw, slaw); –ow (slow, crow, low); –ock (sock, lock, rock); –ack (rack, sack)

Transfer: jaw, glow, clock, shock, track

Making Words Letters: a, i, g, k, l, n, w ("secret" word: walking)

Make: in, win, ink/kin, wig, wag, walk, wing, wink, king, link, nail, waking, walking

Sort: –in (in, win, kin); –ink (ink, wink, link); –ing (king, wing)

Transfer: spin, drink, pink, zing

Making Words Letters: i, o, g, k, n, r, w
("secret" word: working)

Make: in, win, kin, ink, rink, ring, king, wing, wink, work, worn, wrong, rowing, working

Sort: –in (in, win, kin); –ink (ink, rink, wink); –ing (ring, king, wing)

Transfer: spin, shrink, rink, bring

GUESS THE COVERED WORD

Write the sentences below on an overhead transparency or piece of chart paper. (Write the name of a student on each line. This makes the activity even more fun!) Cover the bold word in each sentence with two, dark colored self-stick notes—one note to cover the "onset" (all of the consonants before the first vowel) and the other note to cover the "rime" (the rest of the word). Let students have four guesses and write these guesses on the transparency or chart paper. Then, uncover the onset. Let students guess again, if necessary. Students will use context clues, beginning letters (onsets), and word length to guess the covered words in these sentences.

THINGS TO DO IN A CITY

1. _____ likes to go to the **park**.

2. _____ likes to go to the **movies**.

3. _____ likes to go to the **museum**.

4. _____ likes to go to the **zoo**.

5. _____ likes to **shop**.

CITIES

WRITING

In this mini-lesson, write some things you do when visiting a large city. (In the teacher-written example, the subject is New York City.) As you write, share some things you might do in the city and remember to talk about some things you know to do when writing. Talk about how you begin each sentence with a capital letter and end each sentence with a period. Talk about what you are going to tell about the city and why. Your piece can be real or imaginary.

Here is what a teacher wrote for a second- or third-grade class about a real trip to New York City.

New York City

Each year in November, I visit New York City. My daughter and I fly there early on a Friday morning. We check into our hotel and then head out for lunch and shopping. We usually go to a Broadway show at night. On Saturday, we shop again and visit Soho, Little Italy, and Chinatown. Sunday is always a quiet time. We might have brunch in Central Park, take a subway ride to a favorite place, or go on a harbor tour. We usually come home with many packages and memories. We really enjoy our yearly visit to New York City!

For first grade, you might write a simpler story.

New York City

I like to go to New York City. I always shop and see a Broadway show. I like to visit Soho, Little Italy, and Chinatown. I also like to ride the subway and take taxis. I always come home with packages. I like to visit New York City!

The idea is to write a piece that most students in your class are capable of writing— something they see as a possibility for them. Your example should not be something only you are capable of writing! Remember that in the primary grades, many students need more than one day to create a good piece of writing about a subject.

QUICK WRITES OR OTHER IDEAS FOR WRITING MINI-LESSONS

Here are a few Quick Writes that can be posted in the room so that children will have writing activities to work on. These ideas also could be used for other mini-lessons while learning about cities.

- Write a make-believe story about meeting a famous athlete or movie star on a trip to a big city.

- After you get to the city, you go to the top floor of a large skyscraper. Write about what you see from the top of the building.

- Write about an animal that lives in the city.

CITIES

ART ACTIVITY

A CITY MURAL

MATERIALS

- Bulletin board paper (white, blue, or light brown)
- Pencils
- Markers

Cut a piece of bulletin board paper the size of your bulletin board. Divide the class into different groups: one group will draw buildings; one group will draw the city park; one group will draw vehicles (taxis, cars, delivery trucks, etc.); and one group will draw people in the park and on city streets. The groups can work at different times or all together.

FOOD ACTIVITY

CULTURAL FOODS

All cities are full of ethnic food—pizza and pasta from Italy, salads and baklava from Greece, bratwurst and Wiener schnitzel from Germany, fish and chips from England, curried dishes from India, pastries from Paris, etc. If you have some parents who can help with special ethnic foods, ask them to use their talents to make treats for the class. If not, a trip to the grocery store can produce the same results. Choose one treat or food for the class to make—special cookies are fun to make and eat, as are dishes with rice and vegetables.

Caution: Before completing any food activity, ask families' permission and inquire about students' food allergies and religious or other food preferences.

CULMINATING ACTIVITY

BIG CITY FIELD TRIP

- Ride on a trolley car or bus, visit the library or a museum, and eat in a nearby pizzeria.

- Or, watch a movie or video about a big city in the classroom—it can be a teacher-made production that was filmed in a city. You could also share pictures from a special trip to a big city using a computer and slide show software to create a presentation for all to see and enjoy.

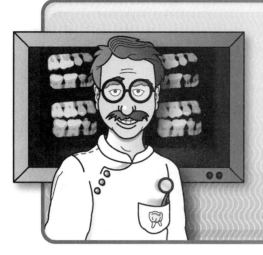

GOING TO THE DENTIST

Few words evoke more anxiety in people than the word dentist. Children can and will pick up on adults' anxiety. Teachers, parents, and dentists all play important roles in making dental visits positive experiences. It is perfectly normal for children to be fearful of going to the dentist, but hearing and reading about other children's experiences can make the visit easier and more rewarding. Knowing the different employees in a dentist's office can help ease anxiety, too. Most children are unaware that the person they spend the most time with is the dental hygienist. Learning about the dentist and what happens at the dentist's office are important steps to help young students develop positive attitudes about going to the dentist.

SELF-SELECTED READING

Books for teachers to read aloud and then put in book baskets or on shelves for Self-Selected Reading:

FICTION

Little Rabbit's Loose Tooth by Lucy Bate (Dragonfly Books, 1988)
After finally losing a tooth, Little Rabbit skeptically awaits a visit from the tooth fairy.

Just Going to the Dentist by Mercer Mayer (Golden Books, 2001)
Little Critter's first visit to the dentist isn't so bad, even though it includes getting a shot and a cavity filled. Parents of children who are preparing to embark on their first dental visits will appreciate this book.

Open Wide! by Tom Barber (Chrysalis Books Group, 2005)
Dr. Murgatroyd, the dentist, has his hands full with Sam, his patient who is hiding under the dentist's chair. The dentist explains that he has had many nervous patients before: a hippo with a toothache, a beaver who nibbles, a goat who wants to eat her chair, and a crocodile with her babies in tow! Sam not only laughs so hard that he opens his mouth, he also learns there is much to be gained by visiting the dentist—Sam gets stickers as a treat.

GOING TO THE DENTIST

Doctor De Soto by William Steig (Farrar, Straus and Giroux, 1990)
Doctor De Soto and his wife are both mice, and they are also dentists who accept all kinds of animals as patients. But, since they are mice, they draw the line at foxes! They make one exception for a pitiful fox who needs to have a rotten tooth extracted and replaced. When the fox is overcome by the thought of a tasty morsel, Dr. De Soto's brilliant plan saves his life—and his dental practice.

Dr. Jekyll, Orthodontist by Dan Greenburg (Grossett & Dunlap, 1997)
There's something strange about Zack's new dentist! Dr. Jekyll insists that Zack drink the mouthwash instead of spitting it out. Zack begins to notice that his teeth are getting more crooked and that Dr. Jekyll seems to be undergoing a transformation of his own. What IS this strange mouthwash, anyway?

Young Cam Jansen and the Lost Tooth by David A. Adler (Puffin Books, 1999)
Cam Jansen, the young sleuth, uses her photographic memory when Annie's tooth falls out in the school art room and promptly disappears. Cam uses her memory and powers of deductive reasoning to recover the lost tooth.

NONFICTION OR INFORMATIONAL BOOKS

What's It Like to Be a Dentist? by Judith Stamper (Simon & Schuster Children's Publishing, 1991)
This book describes daily activities that take place at the dentist's, including examining, cleaning, and X-raying a patient's teeth.

What to Expect When You Go to the Dentist by Heidi E. Murkoff (HarperFestival, 2002)
Going to the dentist is less scary and more fun for today's children! This book explores the routines of dental office visits, the purposes of different tools, and how to practice good dental care.

A Day in the Life of a Dentist by Heather Adamson (Capstone Press, 2003)
Follow a dentist as she prepares for her day, cares for patients, and even eats her lunch. In addition to explanations of tools and procedures, a clock is included on every page to help young readers track the time it takes for the dentist to do different parts of her job.

When I See My Dentist by Susan Kuklin (Simon & Schuster Children's Publishing, 1988)
Photographs show young readers what it's like to go for a checkup at a dentist's office. Hard words are spelled phonetically and defined, and the mystery is taken out of tools and procedures.

GOING TO THE DENTIST

GUIDED READING

Molly and the Slow Teeth by Pat Ross (Houghton Mifflin Company, 1992) is a trade book that also appears in some basal readers.

BEFORE READING

To help build background knowledge, make a chart for lost teeth and let students graph how many teeth they have lost. Discuss the different ways their teeth have come out.

Name	# Lost	How Lost
Tasha	2	pulled
Joe	1	in food
Carlita	3	string on a doorknob
Matt	0	still waiting

VOCABULARY

Introduce the following vocabulary by playing charades.

- wiggle
- budge
- looser
- wobbled
- tongue
- secret

Tell students all of the words are related to losing a tooth. You can act out the words or have students do it. Write the words on the board as students guess them.

DURING READING (PARTNER READING)

Ahead of time, cut out a tooth pattern and make enough copies for half of your class. For example, if you have 22 students, make 11 teeth. Cut each tooth in half like a jigsaw puzzle. Give the left halves to the best readers and the right halves to the struggling readers. Have students find their partners. Instruct them to read in designated areas in their "whisper voices" once they have found their partners.

AFTER READING (COMPREHENSION DISCUSSION)

Have students discuss the following points from the story with their partners:

1. What is the problem? (Molly is the only one in her class that hasn't lost a tooth.)

2. What does she do to solve her problem? (She tries to pull out a tooth; she tries to trick the tooth fairy; and she colors a tooth black.)

3. Does she solve her problem? (After she forgets about it, she loses her tooth in an apple.)

4. Tell your partner about losing your teeth.

Bring all of the students together and let them discuss their answers with the whole class.

GOING TO THE DENTIST

WORKING WITH WORDS

MAKING WORDS

In these lessons, you dictate words, and students use small letter cards (or cut apart letter strips) to make these words. (The "secret" word is the last word made and uses all of the letters.) Next, lead students to sort the words for beginning sounds or spelling patterns. The final step is the transfer step. Have students use the sort patterns to decode and spell new words.

Making Words Letters: e, i, d, n, s, t, t ("secret" word: dentist)

Make: it, in, sit, sin, tin, ten, den/end, dent, tent, sent, send/ends/dens, tend, tens, tide, side, stint, tends, dentist

Sort: –it (it, sit); –in (sin, tin); –ent (dent, tent, sent); –end (end, send, tend); –ide (tide, side)

Transfer: hit, pin, rent, lend, ride,

Making Words Letters: i, u, b, g, h, n, r, s ("secret" word: brushing)

Make: us, bus, bun, run, rug, gun, hug, rub, grub, sing/sign, ring, rush, bring, brush/ shrub, rushing, brushing

Sort: –us (us, bus); –un (bun, run, gun); –ing (sing, ring, bring); suffix –ing (rushing, brushing); –ub (rub, grub, shrub)

Transfer: Gus, stun, sting, stinging

Making Words Letters: a, e, i, i, c, s, t, v ("secret" word: cavities)

Make: is, it, at, sat, sit, set, vet, cat/act, cast/ cats, vast, save, cave, vase, vest, ties, cities, active, cavities

Sort: –it (it, sit); –et (set, vet); –ave (save, cave); –ast (cast, vast)

Transfer: wit, pet, slave, past

© CARSON-DELLOSA • INTEGRATING READING, WRITING, AND WORDS LESSONS • CD-104194

GOING TO THE DENTIST

GUESS THE COVERED WORD

Write the sentences below on an overhead transparency or piece of chart paper. Cover the bold word in each sentence with two, dark colored self-stick notes—one note to cover the "onset" (all of the consonants before the first vowel) and the other note to cover the "rime" (the rest of the word). Let students have four guesses and write these guesses on the transparency or chart paper. Then, uncover the onset. Let students guess again, if necessary. Students will use context clues, beginning letters (onsets), and word length to guess the covered words in these sentences.

CARING FOR YOUR TEETH

1. The dentist **checks** your teeth.

2. You need to **brush** three times a day to promote good dental health.

3. You need your teeth to **chew**.

4. Be sure to eat plenty of healthy **snacks**.

5. The hygienist **cleans** your teeth.

6. You need to brush and floss daily to keep your teeth free of **cavities**.

WRITING

When you learn about people and places and then write about them for students, you are teaching them to write informational pieces. Read aloud a nonfiction book about going to the dentist or being a dentist or dental hygienist. Then, have students offer sentences about the many things they heard and learned. Write their responses on chart paper or sentence strips, writing large enough for students to see and read the words. During this time, you shouldn't correct grammar; instead, simply capture and write students' words. Next, cut the chart paper into individual sentences. With students' help, tape the sentence strips into the correct sequence. Then, with the class, read the sentences out loud in the order they were in the book. Use the correctly sequenced sentences to write a piece for a mini-lesson. Then, guide students to help you add details where they are needed. It is important to model repeatedly how to write a better piece by adding details.

GOING TO THE DENTIST

DAY 1
FIRST DRAFT

Dentists have to go to school.

They work in offices.

They fix broken teeth.

They clean your teeth for you.

They give you stickers, toys, and toothbrushes when you are done.

DAY 2
MAKING IT BETTER

Dentists have to go to school for about eight years. They work in offices with at least one dental hygienist. They see the patients in different rooms. If you fall off your bike and chip a tooth, a dentist will fix your broken tooth. A dentist can also clean your teeth with shiny tools and a spinning toothbrush. Sometimes the dentist lets you pick the flavor of the toothpaste. When the dentist is done, your teeth feel clean. If you were brave, you might get a prize. A dentist might give you stickers, toys, and a toothbrush. You can often pick the kind of toothbrush you like best.

QUICK WRITES OR OTHER IDEAS FOR WRITING MINI-LESSONS

Here are a few Quick Writes that can be posted in the room so that children will have writing activities to work on. These ideas also could be used for other mini-lessons while learning about the dentist.

- Tell how you take care of your teeth.

- Tell about a time you visited the dentist.

- Write a letter to the Tooth Fairy.

FOOD ACTIVITY

APPLE SMILES

INGREDIENTS

- Red apples
- Peanut butter
- Marshmallows

Caution: Before completing any food activity, ask families' permission and inquire about students' food allergies and religious or other food preferences.

DIRECTIONS

1. Slice a red apple into eighths.

2. Have students spread peanut butter on each apple slice.

3. Let students add marshmallow "teeth" to make smiles.

GOING TO THE DENTIST

ART ACTIVITY

PAPER PLATE MOUTHS

MATERIALS

- Paper plates
- Markers or crayons
- Yarn
- Scissors

DIRECTIONS

1. Tell each student to fold a paper plate in half so that it resembles a mouth that can open and close.

2. Have students color the inside of their plates red or pink leaving the outside edge white.

3. Then, tell them to cut slits in the white outside edge to represent teeth.

4. Give students pieces of yarn to use to practice flossing between the "teeth" on their paper plate mouths.

CULMINATING ACTIVITY

DENTIST VISIT

Invite a dentist or dental hygienist into the classroom to discuss his job, explain how to take care of teeth, and answer any questions students may have.

FISH AND FISHING

Many people eat fish—tuna fish, codfish, fish sticks, salmon, catfish, flounder, etc. Often, the only way some students see fish is when it is ready to eat without eyes, tail, scales, or fins. Some children have no experiences seeing fish in their natural habitats or watching them swim. Other children have gone fishing with family members, have held fish and examined them, and can tell you about their scales, tails, and fins. These same children might know which local fish people prefer to eat, how best to catch these fish, how to clean and fillet a fish once it is caught, and even how to cook fish. Going to a pond, lake, or stream and having those experiences with fish is the best way to learn more. But, if that is not possible, there are many wonderful stories about fish and some interesting informational books that can help students increase their background knowledge.

SELF-SELECTED READING

Books for teachers to read aloud and then put in book baskets or on shelves for Self-Selected Reading:

FICTION

Fish Story by Katherine Andres (Simon & Schuster, 1993)
One day, Craig goes fishing and meets a very big fish who gives him one wish. What does Craig choose?

Kumak's Fish: A Tall Tale from the Far North by Michael Bania (Alaska Northwest Books, 2004)
This is a humorous story of a native family in the Arctic and their fishing trip. Using his uncles' hooking stick, Kumak feels a tug and nearly gets pulled into the water. Readers will enjoy the cooperative ending to this charming story.

Salmon Princess: An Alaska Cinderella Story by Mindy Dwyer (Paws IV Publishing, 2004)
This Cinderella story is set in the "Last Frontier," and includes an eagle spirit instead of a fairy godmother and a fishing boot instead of a glass slipper.

Fishing Day by Andrea Davis Pinkney (Jump at the Sun, 2003)
A fishing trip to the Jim Crow River is the setting for this book, which tells the wonderful story of children who can see more than the color of a person's skin.

A Good Day's Fishing by James Prosek
(Simon & Schuster Children's Publishing, 2004)
In beautiful watercolor style, a boy relates all
of the things needed for a good day of fishing,
including good weather, proper equipment,
and his best fishing hat. Includes a glossary.

Anansi Goes Fishing retold by Eric Kimmel
(Holiday House, 1993)
In a variation of this traditional West African
tale, Anansi the spider is outsmarted by his
turtle friend who cons him into doing all of
the work and reaping none of the benefits of a
joint fishing expedition.

Thomas Goes Fishing by the Reverend
W. Awdry (Random House Books for Young
Readers, 2005)
Thomas the Tank Engine longs to go fishing.
It looks like such fun! One day, he complains
to his driver that his boiler hurts. His driver
refills it with water from the river and some
unsuspecting fish. Thomas, the driver, and
the children Thomas has befriended are then
able to enjoy some fishing after all.

Just Fishing with Grandma by Gina Mayer
(Golden Books, 2003)
Little Critter's Grandma volunteers to take
him fishing. Their catch may be small, but
their day of fun is enormous. This book would
be an equally delightful addition to a unit
about grandparents.

A Million Fish . . . More or Less by
Pat McKissack (Dragonfly Books, 1996)
Hugh Thomas, a young boy from the bayou,
goes fishing and meets up with Papa-Daddy
and Elder Abbajon who don't hesitate to
describe their wild adventures on the bayou.
In the true spirit of fish stories, young Hugh
catches his share of fish and then some, but
then he recalls all of the strange and powerful
creatures who wanted to share in the take.

The Big Fish: An Alaskan Fairy Tale by
Marie Wakeland (Misty Mountain, 1993)
This tale about a little girl's perseverance
in trying to catch a king salmon has funny
moments, beautiful illustrations, and the
added bonus of taking place in an unusual
setting—the far North.

NONFICTION OR INFORMATIONAL BOOKS

Kids' Incredible Fishing Stories by Shaun Morey (Workman Publishing Company, 1996)
Think kids never catch big fish? Think again! Lifetime fisherman and author Shaun Morey describes true tales of amazing kids and their amazing catches. Photographs lend authenticity to these stories about the ones that didn't get away.

What's It Like to Be a Fish? by Wendy Pfeffer (HarperTrophy, 1996)
Goldfish take center stage in this book about how fish breathe, eat, swim, and rest. While other fish are mentioned briefly, children will be able to apply the information about goldfish to other fish, as well. This book also includes instructions for setting up a goldfish tank.

The Ocean Alphabet Board Book by Jerry Pallotta (Charlesbridge Publishing, 1986)
Dive into the northern part of the Atlantic Ocean and meet animals and fish whose names begin with the letters A–Z. The illustrations accurately depict all kinds of underwater life.

My Visit to the Aquarium by Aliki (HarperTrophy, 1996)
Can't get to the ocean? Visit this (seemingly) enormous aquarium complete with many different habitats, such as tide pools and freshwater, as well as more unusual ones like a coral reef and a kelp jungle. A tour guide with fish earrings and a visit to the gift shop (to buy this book!) are also included in the storyline.

What Is a Fish? by Robert Sneeden (Sierra Club Books for Children, 1997)
Amazing photographs, often set on white backgrounds, show off these colorful and amazing creatures. Sneeden introduces different types of fish and fish facts, including how they eat, sleep, breathe, and breed.

Fish Tales! by Nat Segaloff and Paul Erickson (Sterling Publishing Company, Inc., 1990)
This book introduces readers to the diversity of ocean life, and it lists the physical characteristics, habitats, and behaviors of various fish.

Fish by Steve Parker (DK Children, 2000)
Photographs and anatomical drawings depict fish and explain important facts, such as how they have evolved and characteristics that make different fish unique.

FISH AND FISHING

GUIDED READING: FICTION

Swimmy by Leo Lionni (Dragonfly Books, 1973) is the story of a small fish in the ocean who is bothered by a big fish. Swimmy, the small fish, asks lots of other small fish to swim in a group with him. By cooperating, they outsmart the big fish.

BEFORE READING

Take a picture walk through this book with students. Talk about what is happening on each page. Ask, "What do you think the story will be about?" (predicting). Talk about the fish (characters), the ocean (setting), and what happened in the beginning and at the end of the book. (Many students can accurately predict the whole story by taking a picture walk.)

DURING (ECHO READING)

Read the text aloud one page at a time and then let students become your echo, reading what you read. If there is enough time (this can wait until tomorrow), students may want to read the story again—silently by themselves or whisper reading with partners.

AFTER READING

Talk about what happened in this story. Were students' predictions correct? If any students have been fishing, ask if they have seen fish swimming in schools. Explain that **school** is the name for a group of fish. Help students make text-to-self connections.

GUIDED READING: NONFICTION

What's It Like to Be a Fish? by Wendy Pfeffer (HarperTrophy, 1996) is a book many second-semester first graders and most second and third graders can read and learn from.

BEFORE READING

A fish is made perfectly to live in water. Find out what students know about a fish's body shape and parts—fins, scales, gills, how it swims, etc. Have students gone fishing with their mothers or fathers? Does Grampy or Grandma take them fishing? Do they have fish bowls or aquariums at home? Begin a KWL chart by finding out what students **K**now about fish and filling in the K column. Ask what students **W**onder or **W**ant to learn about fish and fill in the W column.

DURING READING (INDEPENDENT OR PARTNER READING)

Let students read the book silently by themselves or whisper reading with partners. Give students self-stick notes to mark pages and write new facts they learn. Have them list on the self-stick notes at least three new things they learned while reading the book.

FISH AND FISHING

AFTER READING

Discuss what students **L**earned from the book. Make a list in the L column of the different facts children wrote on their self-stick notes. Here are some facts you might hear:

- Fish live in water—lakes, ponds, oceans, aquariums, etc.

- A fish's body is perfect for swimming.

- A fish has fins to help it swim, steer, and stop.

- Fish breathe with their gills.

- Fish need food; they eat in the water.

- Big fish eat smaller fish.

- Fish's eyes are always open.

- Directions for setting up a goldfish bowl are on pages 30–31.

WORKING WITH WORDS

MAKING WORDS

In these lessons, you dictate words, and students use small letter cards (or cut apart letter strips) to make these words. (The "secret" word is the last word made and uses all of the letters.) Next, lead students to sort the words for beginning sounds or spelling patterns. The final step is the transfer step. Have students use the sort patterns to decode and spell new words.

Making Words Letters: i, o, d, f, g, l, s, h ("secret" word: goldfish)

Make: is, his, hid, lid, old, gold, sold, fold, fish, dish, goldfish

Sort: –id (hid, lid); –old (old, gold, sold, fold); –ish (fish, dish, goldfish)

Transfer: skid, mold, scold, swish

Making Words Letters: i, i, f, g, h, n, s ("secret" word: fishing)

Make: if, in, fin, fig, fins, figs, fish, sing/sign, finish, fishing

Sort: begins with f (fin, fins, figs, fish, finish, fishing); –in (in, fin); plurals (fins, figs)

Transfer: tin, twin, twins

Making Words Letters: e, o, u, d, f, l, n, r ("secret" word: flounder)

Make: on/no, one, den/Ned, led, fed, fun, run, under, flour, flounder

Sort: –ed (Ned, led, fed); –un (fun, run)

Transfer: Ted, wed, gun, sled

FISH AND FISHING

ROUNDING UP THE RHYMES

Read the book *One Fish Two Fish Red Fish Blue Fish* by Dr. Seuss (Random House Books for Young Readers, 1960). "Round up," or find, approximately 10 sets of rhyming pairs from the book. Don't try to do the whole book. Dr. Seuss uses too many rhymes in his books to round up all of the rhymes in any one book!

Here is an example lesson for pages 5–13 of *One Fish Two Fish Red Fish Blue Fish*. (Most of the pages aren't numbered; page 8 is, so these numbers are based on that.)

p. 5	p. 8	p. 11
star	fat	my
car	hat	by
are		

p. 6	p. 9	p. 12
blue	there	four
new	anywhere	more

p. 7	p. 10	p. 13
bad	run	say
bad	fun	way
dad	sun	

Next, call students' attention to the spelling patterns—how the rhymes are written. Eliminate any words that do not have the same spelling pattern. It will look like this:

p. 5	p. 8	p. 11
star	fat	my
car	hat	by
~~are~~		

p. 6	p. 9	p. 12
~~blue~~	there	~~four~~
~~new~~	anywhere	~~more~~

p. 7	p. 10	p. 13
bad	run	say
bad	fun	way
dad	sun	

Now, you have rimes that rhyme! Use these spelling patterns to read and write some transfer words.

READING TRANSFER

Show students the following words, one at a time, written on index cards: **jar**, **slat**, **shy**. Show the words to students; don't say them. For each word, ask students, "What if I were reading and came to this word? Which words on the chart would help me read it?" If students can't read the words on the cards, then hold each card beneath the words with the same pattern and read down (for example, **star**, **car**, **jar**).

WRITING TRANSFER

Ask students, "What if it was writing time and I wanted to write **stay**? Which of the words on the chart would help me write **stay**? Yes, s-a-y and w-a-y." Have students spell **try** and **flat** as you say each word to them. If students can't spell these words, write them on index cards. Then, hold each card beneath the words with the same pattern and read it.

FISH AND FISHING

GUESS THE COVERED WORD

Write the sentences below on an overhead transparency or piece of chart paper. (Write the name of a student on each line. This makes the activity even more fun!) Cover the bold word in each sentence with two, dark colored self-stick notes—one note to cover the "onset" (all of the consonants before the first vowel) and the other note to cover the "rime" (the rest of the word). Let students have four guesses and write these guesses on the transparency or chart paper. Then, uncover the onset. Let students guess again, if necessary. Students will use context clues, beginning letters (onsets), and word length to guess the covered words in these sentences.

WHAT WE LEARNED ABOUT FISH

1. _____ learned that fish have **fins**.

2. _____ learned that fish live in **lakes**.

3. _____ learned that fish eat **worms**.

4. _____ learned that some fish are **colorful**.

5. _____ likes to eat **catfish**.

USING WORDS YOU KNOW

This lesson is fun to do at any grade level (first, second, or third) and will help all students in your class move forward in their decoding ability. Buy a bag of Goldfish® crackers. Use the bag full or empty (if you choose to eat them first!).

1. Hold up the bag. Ask students, "Do you recognize the bag and the crackers? Do you eat them? Do you like them? Can you read the name on the bag?"

2. Write the words **gold** and **fish** on the board, a piece of chart paper, or an overhead transparency.

3. Help students notice the spelling patterns in each word and underline the spelling patterns: **–old** and **–ish**.

4. Write the following words under the appropriate words (gold or fish): **dish, bold, mold, wish, fold, hold, squish, cold**. Have students read the words.

5. Have students write the following words at their desks as you say them: **swish, sold, told, Trish**.

6. If you have second- or third-grade students, try reading and writing some two-syllable words, like **selfish, billfold, blindfold,** and **unselfish**.

FISH AND FISHING

WRITING

A Writing mini-lesson should be written in front of the class on piece of chart paper or an overhead transparency. This mini-lesson is based on things (facts) students have learned about fish. The purpose of this lesson is to model for the class how to write an informational piece. As you write, share some things you know about fish and some things you know about writing. Here is what a finished mini-lesson piece might look like in second or third grade.

Fish

Fish are animals that live in water. Their bodies are made to live underwater and swim. Fish live in oceans, lakes, ponds, and aquariums. Fish eat plants and fish smaller than they are. Some people like to go fishing and catch fish. They fish from the water's edge, from boats, and off of piers. After they catch the fish, they cook or sell them. Fish are healthy food for people to eat.

In first grade, the piece would be simpler. The idea is to write like many students in the class can write.

Fish

Fish live in water. Some people like to catch fish. They use fishing poles. After they catch fish, they eat them!

QUICK WRITES OR OTHER IDEAS FOR WRITING MINI-LESSONS

Here are a few Quick Writes that can be posted in the room so that children will have writing activities to work on. These ideas also could be used for other mini-lessons while learning about fish.

- Tell about a fishing trip, real or imaginary.

- Tell about a visit to an aquarium.

- Imagine being a fish. Describe one day in your life.

FOOD ACTIVITY

If you know someone who fishes, perhaps that person can share how to fillet a fish and cook it. If not, you can buy a fish at a fish market or local grocery store, talk about the many parts of the fish, and then cook the fish. Or, to make it easier, serve fish sandwiches or fish sticks. (Plan this lesson for a day the cafeteria is serving fish sticks or fish sandwiches or visit a nearby fast-food restaurant.)

For dessert, serve fish-shaped candy. Or, make fish-shaped sugar cookies, rolling out premade dough and using fish-shaped cookie cutters. Sprinkle with colorful sugar and bake.

Caution: Before completing any food activity, ask families' permission and inquire about students' food allergies and religious or other food preferences.

FISH AND FISHING

ART ACTIVITY

FISH MURAL

MATERIALS

- Large blue construction paper
- Variety of colorful paint
- Variety of colorful paper
- Scissors
- Glue
- Paintbrushes

DIRECTIONS

1. Give each student a piece of construction paper to use for her background.

2. Encourage students to use a variety of colorful paints and paper to make fish. Tell them to think of tropical fish with colorful lines and spots.

3. Proudly display the fish murals so that everyone can see and admire them.

CULMINATING ACTIVITY

FISH FUN DAY

- Show a fish-related video or movie (for example, *Finding Nemo*) while students eat "gummy" fish or Goldfish® crackers for a snack.

- Let students go "fishing." Tie a 24" piece of yarn to one end of a ruler. Tie a magnet to the other end of the yarn. Cut several fish out of colorful paper and attach paper clips to the fish's mouths. Write the name of one of the following types of fish on each paper fish—**flounder**, **shark**, **tuna**, **goldfish**, **trout**, and **bass**. Have students take turns using the magnetic fishing pole to catch "fish" and read the words. A student can keep a fish if he can read the name written on it.

GARDENING

Where do vegetables come from? The grocery store! That is what many students think. Those who grow their own vegetables know better, but fewer and fewer children have this experience today. Perhaps that is why many young children don't like to eat as many vegetables as children did in the past. When families grew their own vegetables, children ate vegetables regularly. Some students may have gardens in their backyards or have friends or relatives who garden. Gardening teaches students many things. They get a chance to see the growing cycle firsthand. They also realize that people work hard to grow the food we buy from grocery stores. This theme provides some special moments of realization for those who have not previously had firsthand knowledge of the growing process.

Young children, like adults, like to grow things when given the opportunity. In fact, the "kid" in all of us often finds it fascinating to watch something grow. Give students a lecture on gardening and you'll lose them before you finish the first sentence. Show students something growing in a garden and relate it to their lives and they'll learn without even trying. Gardening teaches students that, even if you fail, you can always start over and try again. Take advantage of different growing seasons to introduce students to the wonders of gardening through literature and writing. Start them on the path to a lifetime of enjoyment in the wonderful world of planting and tending a garden.

GARDENING

SELF-SELECTED READING

Books for teachers to read aloud and then put in book baskets or on shelves for Self-Selected Reading:

FICTION

How Groundhog's Garden Grew by Lynne Cherry (Scholastic, Inc., 2003)
To stop him from stealing from other gardens, Squirrel teaches Little Groundhog all about the growing process, including seed gathering, planting, harvesting, and eating. His friends share in his bounty when Little Groundhog invites them to a Thanksgiving harvest feast.

Corduroy's Garden by Alison Inches (Puffin Books, 2004)
When Corduroy the stuffed bear falls down on his job of watching Lisa's garden, a dog digs up the seeds. Corduroy reseeds the garden, watches it grow, and is very surprised by what grows in the garden.

The Chalk Box Kid by Clyde Robert Bulla (Random House Books for Young Readers, 1987)
Nine-year-old Gregory has recently moved and has to share a room with his uncle who is out of work. He makes the best of his situation by drawing a beautiful garden on the walls of a burned-out chalk factory.

Muncha! Muncha! Muncha! by Candace Fleming (Atheneum/Anne Schwartz Books, 2002)
Mr. McGreely plants the garden he has always dreamed of, then tries to find a way to stop some hungry bunnies from devouring his delicious vegetables.

Messy Bessey's Garden! by Patricia and Fredrick McKissack (Children's Press, 2002)
Bessey knows that spring is the time to plant her garden. As she tends it, she learns that a good gardener must water the plants and pull weeds to help things grow. Bessey's hard work is rewarded with tomatoes, carrots, and pumpkins.

NONFICTION OR INFORMATIONAL BOOKS

The Tiny Seed by Eric Carle (Aladdin, 2001)
The tiny seed and its larger companions take the dangerous journey that comes with replanting. Even though many of the other seeds fall into the ocean or are picked too soon, the tiny seed perseveres and becomes a big flower just in time to send its own tiny seeds on the dangerous journey.

How Do Apples Grow? by Betsy Maestro (HarperTrophy, 1993)
This easy-to-follow book details the life of an apple tree and apple growth from flower to fruit.

From Seed to Plant by Gail Gibbons (Holiday House, 1993)
This book details the life cycle of plants, including reproduction, pollination, seed dispersal, and growth. Also included is a simple project that shows how to grow a bean plant.

GUIDED READING

Growing Vegetable Soup by Lois Elhert (Voyager Books, 1990) comes in small and "big book" versions. If possible, use the big book to do this lesson.

BEFORE READING

Explain to students that they are going to help you start a KWL chart on gardening. Have students brainstorm and list as many vegetables as they can think of. Write them on the board or a piece of chart paper under K for what they **K**now. Review the fact that these are also plants that grow in a garden. Then, talk about what students **W**onder or **W**ant to know about gardening and write their questions under W on the chart.

K	W	L
Gardens need to be watered.	How are seeds different?	
Plants come from seeds.	Do all gardens grow the same way?	

VOCABULARY

Bring in the following objects to use as examples when introducing students to the following vocabulary. For **garden**, use a small dish garden.

- trowel
- shovel
- garden
- gloves
- stake
- seeds
- spade
- dirt

Write the words on index cards and have students match the cards to the objects.

Finally, introduce students to the text by taking a Picture Walk. This book is unique because it has a story along with labeled pictures. Have students read and identify the vocabulary with the pictures before reading the story.

DURING READING (SHARED READING)

This is an easy text that can be used for Shared Reading in first and second grades. First, read the book to the class as they listen and look at the illustrations. Then, read it again and invite students to join in and "share" the reading with you.

AFTER READING

Have students discuss what they **L**earned from the story and add those items to the L column of the KWL chart.

K	W	L
Gardens need to be watered.	How are seeds different?	Vegetables grow in gardens.
Plants come from seeds.	Do all gardens grow the same way?	

Have students draw pictures of things they learned from the book. You can also graph students' favorite vegetables to eat or use a Venn diagram to compare and contrast different vegetables or gardening tools.

GARDENING

WORKING WITH WORDS

MAKING WORDS

In these lessons, you dictate words, and students use small letter cards (or cut apart letter strips) to make these words. (The "secret" word is the last word made and uses all of the letters.) Next, lead students to sort the words for beginning sounds or spelling patterns. The final step is the transfer step. Have students use the sort patterns to decode and spell new words.

Making Words Letters: a, e, e, e, b, g, l, s, t, v ("secret" word: vegetables)

Make: get, set, bet, tag, bag, sag, gets, vest, best/bets, save, gave, able, beet, beat, table, stage, beets, beats, stable/tables, vegetables

Sort: –et (get, set, bet); –ab (tab, stab); –est (vest, best); –ag (tag, bag, sag); –able (able, table, stable); homonyms (beat, beet)

Transfer: jet, grab, rest, lag

Making Words Letters: i, o, g, g, n, r, w ("secret" word: growing)

Make: on, or, go, no, now/won, row, Ron, wing, ring, worn, grow, wrong, wring, rowing, growing

Sort: –on (on, Ron); –ing (wing, ring, wring); –ow (row, grow); wr– (wrong, wring); homonyms (ring, wring)

Transfer: Don, bring, stow, wrench

Making Words Letters: a, e, d, g, n, r, s ("secret" word: gardens)

Make: age, sad, sag, rag, red, ear, dear, near, dare, read, rage, sage, snag, grade, reads, snare, grades, garden, gardens

Sort: –ag (sag, rag, snag); –ear (ear, dear, near); –age (age, rage, sage)

Transfer: flag, fear, stage

GUESS THE COVERED WORD

Write the sentences below on an overhead transparency or piece of chart paper. Cover the bold word in each sentence with two, dark colored self-stick notes—one note to cover the "onset" (all of the consonants before the first vowel) and the other note to cover the "rime" (the rest of the word). Let students have four guesses and write these guesses on the transparency or chart paper. Then, uncover the onset. Let students guess again, if necessary. Students will use context clues, beginning letters (onsets), and word length to guess the covered words in these sentences.

For the first lesson, write the name of a student on each line to make the activity even more fun!

FRESH FROM THE GARDEN

1. _____ likes to eat **corn**.

2. _____ likes to eat **zucchini**.

3. _____ likes to eat **radishes**.

4. _____ likes to eat **cucumbers**.

5. _____ likes to eat **tomatoes**.

6. _____ likes to eat **beans**.

PLANTS

1. Plants need **water** to grow.

2. You can eat the **roots** of some plants.

3. **Vegetables** come from seeds.

4. Some plants grow in **gardens**.

5. Seeds come in different **shapes**.

WRITING

WRITING TO INFORM

The purpose of this writing mini-lesson is to teach students to write about something they have learned during the gardening theme. First, write for your students and tell them something you have learned during the theme as you talk about what writers do as they write. Following is an example of a finished piece for a second- or third-grade class.

Gardens are Special

Flowers grow in gardens. Vegetables grow in gardens. Plants grow from seeds. Sometimes they are started inside, and sometimes the seeds are planted right in the garden. Plants need sunshine and water to grow. Radishes, carrots, and potatoes grow underground. Tomatoes, corn, and green beans grow above ground. Gardens need to be watered and weeded. There is nothing that tastes better than food fresh from a garden!

When you finish, ask students to write something they learned about gardens during this theme.

QUICK WRITES OR OTHER IDEAS FOR WRITING MINI-LESSONS:

Here are a few Quick Writes that can be posted in the room so that children will have writing activities to work on. These ideas also could be used for other mini-lessons while learning about gardening.

- Describe the life cycle of a plant.

- Write a story about a plant that talks to you.

- Tell about your favorite kind of plant and why it is your favorite.

FOOD ACTIVITY

"DIRT" CUPS

INGREDIENTS

- Instant chocolate pudding

- 8 oz. paper cups

- "Gummy" worms

- Cream-filled chocolate sandwich cookies, crushed

- Graham crackers, crushed

- Green plastic spoons

1. Let students help you make the chocolate pudding according to the recipe on the box.

2. Give each student a paper cup and let her fill it halfway with pudding. Encourage students to add gummy worms and crushed cream-filled chocolate sandwich cookies.

3. Finally, let students top their mixtures with crushed graham crackers. They can eat their "dirt" with green spoons that look like stems growing from the dirt.

Caution: Before completing any food activity, ask families' permission and inquire about students' food allergies and religious or other food preferences

GARDENING

ART ACTIVITY

FLORAL PENHOLDER

Make floral pens and let students decorate terra-cotta flower pots with latex paint to make penholders.

MATERIALS

- Dry beans
- 4" terra-cotta flower pots
- Artificial flowers
- Ballpoint ink pens
- Floral tape
- Latex paint
- Fine-tip permanent markers

DIRECTIONS

1. Give each student a flowerpot. Let students use paint to decorate the pots with fingerprint caterpillars and bugs. After the paint dries, students can use fine-tip permanent markers to add legs, eyes, and antennae to their critters.

2. Have students fill their flowerpots halfway with dry beans.

3. Give each student one artificial flower and one ballpoint pen. Let students throw away the caps to their pens. Help students use floral tape to attach the flowers to their pens. Remind them to completely cover the stems and pens with tape, leaving only the tip for writing exposed.

4. Tell students to place the pens, writing end down, in their flowerpots. The beans will keep the pens from drying out.

CULMINATING ACTIVITY

VEGETABLE GARDEN

Plant vegetable seeds in the sections of a foam egg carton. Choose six different kinds of vegetables and plant each type of seed in two sections of the egg carton. Make tiny stakes and signs (paper taped to toothpicks) to label the vegetables. Place the egg-carton garden in a sunny spot and water as necessary.

GARDENING

HAVING A PET

Many students dream of owning a pet if they do not have one. Some children want ponies or horses. When they learn that they won't be getting one of those, they usually settle for a dog or cat. It is not difficult to get students interested in wanting pets. However, it is difficult to get them to care for new pets once the initial excitement has worn off. Owning a pet can have many positive outcomes. It can help teach a child responsibility, patience, and the importance of regular routines. Caring for a pet can also help to prepare a child for some major life events, such as sickness and death. Since getting a pet can be a big investment of money and time (especially if a child isn't ready to take care of a pet by herself), it is usually better to start with a simple first pet like a fish, gerbil, or hermit crab. Other slightly more "exotic" options for a first pet might be a small lizard or frog.

It is an enormous responsibility to take good care of a pet. Since it is difficult for children to comprehend this, books are a great way to get the message across. Children can also share their experiences by writing about taking care of a classroom pet, since classrooms are the perfect place to introduce children to pet care. Some great active pets for the classroom are fish, hamsters, gerbils, guinea pigs, rats, mice, or even birds.

SELF-SELECTED READING

Books for teachers to read aloud and then put in book baskets or on shelves for Self-Selected Reading:

FICTION

Bathtime for Biscuit by Alyssa Satin Capucilli (HarperTrophy, 1999)
Everything is ready for Biscuit to take a bath—everything except Biscuit! After rolling in the mud and playing in the garden with his friend Puddles, will Biscuit ever get clean?

Franklin Wants a Pet by Paulette Bourgeois (Scholastic Paperbacks, 1995)
Franklin the turtle wants a pet. When Franklin proves to his parents that he can take care of a pet, they are surprised that he picks a pretty goldfish for his own.

Arthur and the School Pet by Marc Brown (Random House Books for Young Readers, 2003)
Over Christmas vacation, Arthur's little sister D. W. brings home Speedy, the classroom gerbil. D. W. aspires to teach him some new tricks. She quickly finds out that Speedy got his name for a reason and that caring for a pet is a challenge.

Junie B. Jones Smells Something Fishy by Barbara Park (Random House Books for Young Readers, 1998)
Junie B.'s school is having a pet day—for caged animals only. Junie B. can't bring her dog, so she thinks about other possibilities, including a worm and a jar of ants. Finally, she find a solution to her pet problem and becomes the proud owner of a fish stick.

Pinky and Rex and the Just-Right Pet by James Howe (Aladdin, 2002)
Pinky the dog lover wants a dog as a family pet, but everyone else votes to get a cat. When Patches the kitten arrives, Pinky's sister is a little rough with her, and the kitten seeks refuge with the more gentle Pinky.

The Case of the Best Pet Ever by James Preller (Scholastic Paperbacks, 2003)
Jigsaw and his partner Mila are always ready to solve a new mystery. In this book, the pet store is having a pet show for the neighborhood kids. First prize for the most talented pet is a shiny gold medal. But, when the prize disappears, Jigsaw and his dog Rags have to enter the contest themselves so that they can solve the mystery and return the medal to its rightful winner.

Just Me and My Puppy by Mercer Mayer (Golden Books, 1998)
Little Critter has a new puppy his parents will let him keep—if he takes care of it. Little Critter soon finds out that caring for a puppy is very hard work but definitely worth it.

Hachiko Waits by Lesléa Newman (Henry Holt and Company, 2004)
Hachiko Waits is inspired by a true story about the loyalty of man's best friend. In this case, the man is a professor who meets his Akita, named Hachiko, at the train station every day. When his master has a heart attack, the dog continues to wait for 10 more years for his master's return.

NONFICTION OR INFORMATIONAL BOOKS

Should We Have Pets? A Persuasive Text by Sylvia Lollis and Joyce Hogan (Mondo Publishing, 2002)
A second-grade class develops and presents arguments for and against pet ownership. This text is a great introduction to persuasive reading and writing.

My Cat: How to Have a Happy, Healthy Pet by Lynn Cole (Northwood Press, 2001)
A perfect introduction to pet ownership, this book explains the responsibilities and joys of caring for a kitten. Detailed illustrations and photographs are included.

I Love Guinea Pigs by Dick King-Smith (Candlewick Press, 2001)
Guinea pigs are popular pets in many countries. This guide celebrates the chunky, cuddly guinea pig as it answers many questions about this charming pet.

HAVING A PET

Wackiest White House Pets by Gibbs Davis (Scholastic Press, 2004)
Explore the pets that have belonged to U. S. presidents and their families. Some of them are quite surprising. For example, John Quincy Adams's alligator enjoyed chasing the guests! Thomas Jefferson strolled around the garden with his pet grizzly bears! James Buchanan received the gift of a herd of elephants from the King of Siam! Funny anecdotes and hilarious illustrations are included in this interesting and irresistible look at American history.

Hachiko: The True Story of a Loyal Dog by Pamela S. Turner (Houghton Mifflin Company, 2004)
Hachiko, a real dog who lived in Tokyo, waited faithfully for his owner at the Shibuya train station long after his owner died and could not come to meet him. Hachiko became famous in Japan and beyond for his loyalty and was adored by scores of people who passed through the station every day. This is Hachiko's story through the eyes of Kentaro, a young boy whose life is changed forever by his friendship with this very special dog.

GUIDED READING

Arthur's Pet Business by Marc Brown (Little, Brown and Company, 1993) tells how Arthur takes care of pets to earn the money to buy a dog—but he gets one in a different way.

DAY 1
BEFORE READING

List the types of pets that students have or would like to have. Make a class graph. Discuss and write the responsibilities of having a pet. Bring in a class pet and assign different children to care for it daily.

Sing the song "How Much Is That Doggie in the Window?" (words and music by Bob Merrill, Golden Bell Songs, US Music, and Chappell and Co., 1952). Substitute a different pet, adjective, and noun each time you sing it.

For example, the original lyrics say "How much is that doggie in the window? The one with the waggly tail?" Change the lyrics to the "How much is that **kitty** in the window? The one with the **soft, soft fur**?" (or **gerbil** and **wiggly nose**, **snake** and **scaly skin**, etc.). See how many variations students can think of.

VOCABULARY
Introduce the following vocabulary using the Rivet method (page 26):
Have students predict what this Arthur story will be about based on the vocabulary.

- promise
- business
- responsibility
- schedule
- allowed
- strange
- earned

DURING READING (ERT)

Have students read together and use ERT (pages 41–42) to read for the following purposes:

- "Everyone read the first three pages to see what kind of pet Arthur would like to have."

- "This is a two-hander. Everyone read the next two pages to see what Arthur's parents have to say about this and what Arthur's friends suggest he do to show he is responsible."

- "Everyone read the next three pages to find out how Arthur feels his pet business is going."

- "Everyone read the next three pages to see what kind of pet Perky is."

- "This is a two-hander. Everyone read the next two pages to see what Arthur does for Perky and what animals Arthur is to take care of."

- "Everyone read the next page and tell me why Arthur's mom wants the animals to be in the basement."

- "Everyone read the next two pages and tell how Arthur shows he is responsible."

- "Everyone read the next three pages to see why Arthur is in real trouble."

- "Everyone read the next two pages to see where Perky is."

- "Everyone read to the end of the story to find out what Arthur earns from his pet business."

AFTER READING

Discuss the story with students. Then, toss the Beach Ball with the story questions (page 28) for them to answer.

In the story, Arthur designs a sign advertising his pet business. Have students draw signs to advertise pet businesses.

Return to the Before Reading song ("How Much Is That Doggie in the Window?"). Write all of the additional verses students came up with and put them together to make a class book.

WORKING WITH WORDS

MAKING WORDS

In these lessons, you dictate words, and students use small letter cards (or cut apart letter strips) to make these words. (The "secret" word is the last word made and uses all of the letters.) Next, lead students to sort the words for beginning sounds or spelling patterns. The final step is the transfer step. Have students use the sort patterns to decode and spell new words.

Making Words Letters: e, e, i, o, b, l, n, p, r, s, s
("secret" word: responsible)

Make: is, so, no/on, Ron, nip, sip, less, press, bless, lesson, responsible

Sort: –on (on, Ron); –ess (less, press, bless)

Transfer: con, mess

Making Words Letters: a, a, e, e, i, i, n, n, r, r, t, v
("secret" word: veterinarian)

Make: an, tan/ant, ran, van, vet, net, ear, near, rear, rain, vain, vein, rein, rent, vent, rant, tear, nine, vine, enter, veterinarian

Sort: –an (an, tan, ran, van); –et (vet, net); –ain (rain, vain); –ein (rein, vein); –ent (rent, vent); –ear (ear, near, tear); –ine (nine, vine); homonyms (vain, vein; rain, rein)

Transfer: plan, get, rain, spent, fear, spine

Making Words Letters: a, i, i, g, n, n, r, t
("secret" word: training)

Make: in, at, rat/art, tin, gin, gnat, gain, rain, ring, ting, train, grain, raining, training

Sort: –it (it, grit); –at (at, rat, gnat); –in (in, gin, tin); –ain (gain, rain, train, grain); –ing (ring, ting)

Transfer: splat, win, sprain, sling

HAVING A PET

GUESS THE COVERED WORD

Write the sentences below on an overhead transparency or piece of chart paper. Cover the bold word in each sentence with two, dark colored self-stick notes—one note to cover the "onset" (all of the consonants before the first vowel) and the other note to cover the "rime" (the rest of the word). Let students have four guesses and write these guesses on the transparency or chart paper. Then, uncover the onset. Let students guess again, if necessary. Students will use context clues, beginning letters (onsets), and word length to guess the covered words in these sentences.

PETS

1. Taking care of pets is a **huge** responsibility.

2. I **walk** my dog at least twice a day.

3. My brother gives water to our **gerbil**.

4. We keep a **tadpole** in an aquarium.

5. I took my cat to the vet to get a **checkup**.

WRITING

In the primary grades, teachers need to model and teach personal narratives, stories, and informational pieces over and over. Teachers can also prepare written products such as letters. The following activities help students explore this genre.

LETTER WRITING

Getting children interested in writing letters can be difficult, but children will eagerly write with this activity. The White House maintains a Web site for children and one of the links provides information about the White House pets (*http://www.whitehouse. gov/kids/pets/*). Americans have been fascinated with first families' pets for years. Now, children can actually e-mail or write the White House with questions for the pets. A personal aide to the president or the White House Internet director will respond to the questions in a relatively timely fashion. If you send a letter to one of the pets at the White House or even to the president himself to ask about one of the pets, you can almost guarantee a letter back. It is not uncommon to get an autographed picture from one of the pets or even from the president. What a neat way to get kids interested in writing! Here is the address for writing to a pet at the White House:

(Pet's Name)
The White House
1600 Pennsylvania Avenue NW
Washington, DC 20500

HAVING A PET

QUICK WRITES OR OTHER IDEAS FOR WRITING MINI-LESSONS

Here are a few Quick Writes that can be posted in the room so that children will have writing activities to work on. These ideas also could be used for other mini-lessons while learning about pets.

- Describe your pet or a pet you would like to have.

- Tell about the responsibilities of owning a pet.

- What happens when your pet starts "talking" to you? What does it "say"?

FOOD ACTIVITY

PEOPLE TREATS

INGREDIENTS

- Canned refrigerator biscuits

- Butter

- Peanut butter and jelly (optional)

DIRECTIONS

1. Give each student one biscuit and have him form it into the shape of a dog bone.

2. Have students place their bone-shaped biscuits on a cookie sheet and brush them lightly with melted butter.

3. Bake as directed on the biscuit can. Most cafeteria managers will be more than willing to cook things for you as long as you do the project early in the morning, so that the recipe can finish baking before the mad dash to lunch begins.

4. Let students eat their treats while they are still warm. They are great with a little peanut butter and/or jelly!

Caution: Before completing any food activity, ask families' permission and inquire about students' food allergies and religious or other food preferences.

HAVING A PET

ART ACTIVITY

DRAWING PETS

Get a "how-to-draw" book and teach students, step-by-step, how to draw a pet.

CULMINATING ACTIVITY

PET SHOW

- Let students bring in photos of their pets or pets they would like to have.

- Invite a person from the local humane society or animal rescue agency to bring a cat and/or dog to show the class.*

- Introduce a class pet, such as a hermit crab or gerbil. Have students write what needs to be done to take care of the animal. Assign different students to care for it daily.*

- If you know anyone that can make balloon animals, such as dogs, cats, and birds, invite him to class to make balloon pets for students.

- Serve the People Treats (page 85) as a Pet Show snack.

*Caution: Before completing any activity with a real animal, ask families' permission and inquire about students' animal allergies.

MOVING

Moving has become a common event for many families and provides a variety of learning experiences. No matter how often families change residences, moving can trigger a whole range of emotions and situations. One out of five American families moves each year; most of those moves are within the same community or to a neighboring state. Some children never experience a move and spend their entire lives in the same homes. You can help these children build their background knowledge by conducting a unit about moving.

Moving can be an exciting adventure for families as they go to new places, make new friends, and meet new neighbors. Despite all of the excitement and positive moments, moving can also be a challenging and difficult experience. School-aged children often are quite excited about a family move and love to become involved in the planning process. However, families must keep in mind that relationships with peers are very important for school-aged children. Although they can understand the separation from friends and neighbors that is about to happen, they may not have the maturity to deal with their emotions.

At first, children may embrace a move, but a month or so later, many children become quite angry about the move, especially if they have not had much success forming a new group of friends. When reality sets in, they may experience a great deal of confusion, frustration, and anger. You can help with this transition by reading books that let children know they are not the only ones to have these feelings. You can also have children write about their own experiences with moving and share them with the class. Knowing that somebody else has felt the same confusion, frustration, and anger can be very helpful to children.

SELF-SELECTED READING

Books for teachers to read aloud and then put in book baskets or on shelves for Self-Selected Reading:

FICTION

Alexander, Who's Not (Do You Hear Me? I Mean It!) Going to Move by Judith Viorst (Aladdin, 1998)
Alexander's family is moving a thousand miles away. Alexander doesn't want to move away from his best friend, his favorite babysitter, or anything else. He threatens to live in a tree house or cave, but he lets his parents console him eventually.

I'm Not Moving, Mama! by Nancy White Carlstrom (Aladdin, 1999)
Little Mouse protests as Mama packs his favorite things. Mama reassures him at every turn by describing things they will share in their new home. Finally, Little Mouse understands that the most important thing is being together, no matter where.

We Just Moved! by Stephen Krensky (Cartwheel, 1998)
With the exception of some things, such as giants and a moat filled with alligators, moving to a new castle in medieval times is like moving to a new home today. The little boy in the story learns that some things are the same while others are different, and it will take a little time to adjust.

The Berenstain Bears' Moving Day by Stan and Jan Berenstain (Random House Books for Young Readers, 1981)
When the Bear family moves, Brother Bear is happy that he will be able to take his toys and books but sad that he cannot bring his friends. When they arrive, the bears find that the house needs some fixing up, but Brother has a room of his own. He is even happier to see that there are many kids to play with in his new neighborhood.

Henry and Mudge and Annie's Good Move by Cynthia Rylant (Aladdin, 2000)
Annie loves her cousin Henry and his dog Mudge, but even that can't make her feel totally comfortable about moving. Annie is worried and apprehensive about almost everything to do with the move. Henry asks if Annie would like to snuggle under a blanket in the backseat of the car. She eventually falls asleep nestled up to Mudge, feeling comforted. When the move is complete at last, Annie begins to settle in and enjoy living next door.

Amelia's Road by Linda Jacobs Altman (Lee & Low Books, 1995)
Amelia Luisa Martinez is the daughter of migrant farm workers. Weary of moving so often, young Amelia dreams of a permanent home. At the end of the story, she buries a treasure box beneath a tree and vows to come back someday. This book is useful for teaching children about different traditions and ways of life for different families.

Good-Bye, 382 Shin Dang Dong by Frances Park and Ginger Park (National Geographic Children's Books, 2002)
Address the issue of immigrating families with this sensitive story about Jangmi, a young Korean girl who is troubled at the thought of leaving her home at 382 Shin Dang Dong. As she and her family prepare to move to America, their friends throw them a good-bye party. Jangmi and her friend

Kisuni sit under the willow tree in the rain and promise to stay in touch. When Jangmi arrives in Massachusetts, her new house is intimidating at first, but then her familiar belongings arrive, the neighbors bring food to greet them, and Jangmi meets a new friend—a young girl named Mary. By the end of the book, Jangmi feels much better in her new home.

NONFICTION OR INFORMATIONAL BOOKS

Moving by Janine Amos (Gareth Stevens Publishing, 2002)
Amos uses letters written to and by children, scenes of moving, and colorful photographs to help children and their parents understand what it feels like to move. The author includes helpful suggestions for helping children deal with the stresses of moving to a new place.

The Moving Book: A Kids' Survival Book
by Gabriel Davis (First Books, 2003)
This interactive how-to book keeps kids busy and involved in the moving process. Fun activities related to moving include instructions for packing, collecting friends' autographs, getting pets ready to travel, and mapping a new neighborhood. The book is divided into three sections (before, during, and after the move) to help children deal with all phases of moving.

GUIDED READING

Ira Says Goodbye by Bernard Waber (Houghton Mifflin Company, 1988) has a well-known main character and is a good choice for second and third grades. This book could be used around the end of first grade but may need to be divided into two days of reading.

BEFORE READING

Have students brainstorm how they would feel if a friend were moving away. Discuss reasons why people move. Let students share their own text-to-self experiences.

VOCABULARY

Introduce the following vocabulary using the Rivet method (page 26):

* moving
* snort
* thriller

* scoot
* lonely
* surprise

Have students predict what the story will be about based on the vocabulary words.

DURING READING (THREE-RING CIRCUS)

Divide students into three groups: Reading by Themselves, Reading with Partners, and Reading with the Teacher. Post a chart of the assigned groups. Tell students, "Today, we are going to read a story about a boy whose best friend is moving away. We are going to read this story in Three-Ring Circus. Let's look at our chart to see how each of you will be reading *Ira Says Goodbye*."

MOVING

AFTER READING

Lead students in discussing the story and, with their help, fill in the information on a Story Map. (See the categories to the right.) A Story Map is a graphic organizer that helps organize information from stories.

STORY MAP

Title: _____

Author: _____

Setting: _____

Characters: _____

Beginning: _____

Middle: _____

End: _____

Conclusion: _____

WORKING WITH WORDS

MAKING WORDS

In these lessons, you dictate words, and students use small letter cards (or cut apart letter strips) to make these words. (The "secret" word is the last word made and uses all of the letters.) Next, lead students to sort the words for beginning sounds or spelling patterns. The final step is the transfer step. Have students use the sort patterns to decode and spell new words.

Making Words Letters: a, i, c, g, k, n, p ("secret" word: packing)

Make: in, an, can, pan, pin/nip, nap, kin, cap, pack, ping, king, pain, gain, nick, pick, packing

Sort: –an (an, can, pan); –in (in, pin, kin); –ick (nick, pick); –ain (pain, gain)

Transfer: plan, spin, brick, brain

Making Words Letters: a, e, i, g, l, n, v ("secret" word: leaving)

Make: Al, an, van, vine, line, live/evil, lane, give, gain, vein, veil, vane, nail, given, leaving

Sort: –an (an, van); –ive (live, give); –ine (vine, line); homonyms (vane, vein)

Transfer: man, span, shine, mine

Making Words Letters: e, i, o, b, g, g, l, n, n, s ("secret" word: belongings)

Make: no/on, one, big, beg, leg, long, song, gone, bone, lone, none, neon, bones, legs, longs, belong, longing, belongings

Sort: –one (one, none); –one (bone, lone); –ong (long, song, belong); –eg (beg, leg)

Transfer: done, stone, strong, Meg

© CARSON-DELLOSA • INTEGRATING READING, WRITING, AND WORDS LESSONS • CD-104194

GUESS THE COVERED WORD

Write the sentences below on an overhead transparency or piece of chart paper. Cover the bold word in each sentence with two, dark colored self-stick notes—one note to cover the "onset" (all of the consonants before the first vowel) and the other note to cover the "rime" (the rest of the word). Let students have four guesses and write these guesses on the transparency or chart paper. Then, uncover the onset. Let students guess again, if necessary. Students will use context clues, beginning letters (onsets), and word length to guess the covered words in these sentences.

MY FRIEND IS MOVING

1. I feel **miserable** because my friend is moving.

2. My friend wants me to help him pack his **toys**.

3. We are going to send **pictures** each month.

4. We plan to **talk** often.

5. I hope he will like his new **neighborhood**.

WRITING

Explain to students that they will be writing about moving and missing a friend, and they should think about all of the things they know about the topic. Some students have never moved, so they may not have experienced the loss of a friend. If this is the case, they can deviate and write about how they felt when they lost an object (toy, money, gift, etc.).

If students have not had much experience with synonyms, you may need to teach a synonyms mini-lesson before attempting this lesson. If you do decide to teach a synonyms mini-lesson, stay away from words about feelings that might pop up in the actual lesson on leaving a friend.

Have each student start a chart by writing as many words about feelings as she can in the left column. Then, beside each word, have her try to list other words in the column on the right that describe that same feeling. If students are having trouble, have them work in pairs or use thesauruses. Explain that these words are called synonyms.

Name of a Feeling	Synonyms
happy	joyful, cheery, glad
mad	angry, furious, livid
excited	thrilled

Teach a mini-lesson where you draw a picture of yourself moving and leaving a friend. Then, model writing about a time you moved and how you felt.

Have students draw and then write personal narrative pieces about moving and what they felt when they left their friends. They should focus on what caused the feelings, as well as what the feelings caused them to do. Each piece should have a conclusion that explains why and how the feelings eventually changed.

Students in the primary grades are capable of using colorful and descriptive language, but they must get comfortable using those types of words, rather than **good**, **bad**, **happy**, **sad**, **nice**, etc. Children in second and third grades can also begin to use simple thesauruses. As long as the thesauruses are targeted for the appropriate grade levels, they will enhance students' word skills, and you may begin to see students use thesauruses in their editing stages.

QUICK WRITES OR OTHER IDEAS FOR WRITING MINI-LESSONS

Here are a few Quick Writes that can be posted in the room so that children will have writing activities to work on. These ideas also could be used for other mini-lessons while learning about moving.

- How would you feel if one of your friends moved away?

- How would you feel if you had to move away?

- Write a letter to a friend or relative who has moved and whom you have not seen in a while.

FOOD ACTIVITY

NO-BAKE CAKE

In the Guided Reading story (page 89), Ira and his mother bake an angel food cake to help him feel better. Follow this easy recipe and make a cake with your class.

INGREDIENTS

- 1 large can fruit cocktail (or other canned fruit)
- 1 container whipped topping
- 1 box snack cakes (12 count)

DIRECTIONS

1. Cut the snack cakes in half lengthwise and line the bottom of a small cake pan with half of the cake pieces.

2. Spread whipped topping over the snack cake layer.

3. Drain the juice from the can of fruit cocktail and spread the fruit over the whipped topping.

4. Cover the fruit with the rest of the snack cake pieces.

5. Place in the refrigerator until ready to serve.

Caution: Before completing any food activity, ask families' permission and inquire about students' food allergies and religious or other food preferences.

ART ACTIVITY

ADDRESS BOOKS

Have students design their own address books. Assemble books using construction paper for covers and plain paper for the pages. Fold all of the paper from top to bottom and staple along the folded edges to create books. Label the pages with the letters of the alphabet. For a more simple project, provide small composition books and let students design creative covers.

CULMINATING ACTIVITY

FAREWELL PARTY

- Let students sign each other's address books. Have them write their names, addresses, and phone numbers so that they can keep in touch. Each student needs to learn his address and phone number, and this is a fun way to practice. Of course, in some classes, you may need to write the information out and have students cut and paste.

  Note: Be sure to ask families' permission before letting students exchange personal information.

- Serve the No-Bake Cake with juice or water.

MUSEUM VISIT

Museums enrich the lives of students by providing learning opportunities. Most children's museums now have interactive exhibits that are designed to provide children with opportunities to explore, think, face challenges, and develop new understandings of the world around them. Educators and museum directors are guided by research that shows how important constructive play is to the enrichment of children's lives. Most students visit small museums in their local communities with parents, school groups, or community groups. These museum trips support and influence students' educational growth and development. For students who might not otherwise have access to a museum's rich array of resources, reading and writing about museums can help to bridge that gap. Most children simply relate museums to dinosaurs, but museums actually allow children to discover other cultures, manipulate objects, role play, problem solve, and develop eye-hand coordination within a variety of unique exhibits and programs.

SELF-SELECTED READING

Books for teachers to read aloud and then put in book baskets or on shelves for Self-Selected Reading:

FICTION

Cam Jansen and the Mystery of the Dinosaur Bones by David A. Adler (Puffin Books, 2004)
Cam Jansen (of photographic memory fame) takes a tour of a museum and notices that one of the dinosaur's bones are missing. She and her friend Eric set out to catch the bone thief.

Curious George and the Dinosaur (Houghton Mifflin Company, 1989)
Curious George takes a field trip and climbs to the top of a dinosaur skeleton. He manages to entertain a class that is also in the museum.

Pinky and Rex by James Howe (Aladdin, 1998)
Pinky has 27 stuffed animals. His friend Rex has 27 dinosaurs. These two friends manage to maintain their friendship while solving a conflict involving a pink stuffed dinosaur available at a museum gift shop.

Norman the Doorman by Don Freeman (Puffin, 1989)
Norman, a mouse who is a doorman, longs to see the art treasures of his building. His own artistic talent allows him to fulfill his wish.

Harry and the Dinosaurs at the Museum
by Ian Whybrow (Random House Books for Young Readers, 2005)
Harry joins his big sister Sam on a museum trip with their grandmother. When Sam gets lost, he entertains himself by introducing his bucket of plastic dinosaurs to their giant, skeletal ancestors.

Trapped in the Museum of Unnatural History by Dan Greenburg (Rebound by Sagebrush, 2002)
Zack lives in New York City and loves visiting the Museum of Natural History. When he is separated from his class and trapped in the museum overnight, he finds out what a spooky place it can be.

Katie and the Mona Lisa by James Mayhew (Orchard Books, 1999)
While on a museum visit with her grandmother, Katie steps into a painting and meets the Mona Lisa, who has lost her smile. Katie and the woman from the painting embark on a tour of other paintings so that Mona Lisa can regain her famous smile.

Miss Malarkey's Field Trip by Judy Finchler (Walker Books for Young Readers, 2004)
Brave Miss Malarkey takes her class to the science museum. Her rowdy students enjoy the field trip as their teacher's headache steadily worsens.

NONFICTION OR INFORMATIONAL BOOKS

Visiting the Art Museum by Laurene Kransy Brown and Marc Brown (Puffin Books, 1990)
A family takes a visit to the art museum, where they see examples of paintings by various artists such as Cassatt, Cézanne, Picasso, Pollock, Renoir, Rousseau, Van Gogh, and Warhol, as well as primitive and historically significant pieces. Funny comments from family members are included in speech bubbles. This is a nice introduction for children who are preparing to visit a museum.

Working at a Museum by Arthur John L'Hommedieu (Children's Press, 1999)
Working at a Museum tells about the different responsibilities of people who work at the Brooklyn Children's Museum. Readers will learn about a variety of careers that are necessary to keep the museum functioning smoothly, including educators, events managers, public relations staff, and even security officers.

Out and About at the Science Center by Kitty Shea (Picture Window Books, 2004)
Shea takes readers on a fun field trip by describing things they will see at a science center or museum, such as displays about dinosaurs or the human body or space. This is a helpful book to read to students before a field trip because it also covers what is acceptable behavior when visiting a museum or any similar place.

MUSEUM VISIT

GUIDED READING

Curious George and the Dinosaur (Houghton Mifflin Company, 1989) is a good book for the end of first grade and early second grade. *Cam Jansen and the Mystery of the Dinosaur Bones* by David A. Adler (Puffin Books, 2004) is a good choice for third grade. Both books are about dinosaur exhibits at a museum and have pictures to help students make predictions before reading. The following activities could be done with either book, depending on students' reading levels.

BEFORE READING

Construct a Story Map Wheel by dividing a cardboard circle into six sections. Label the sections as follows:
1. The title of the book and author; 2. The characters; 3. The setting; 4. The problem; 5. The solution or ending; 6. Connections. Use a paper fastener to mount the circle on a piece of cardboard so that it spins.

Talk to students about going on field trips and the rules they must remember on the bus and when visiting places. Let students take a picture walk through the book to see where Jimmie's class (or Cam's class) goes on their field trip and who goes along. Let students predict what will happen and how the story will end. Write several predictions on the board or chart paper. Show students the Story Map Wheel and read what it says in each section. Tell them they will discuss the answers for each section with their partners when they finish reading.

DURING READING (PARTNER READING)

Divide the class into partners and have them read alternating pages. Partners can read at desks or anywhere "around the room." Students love to to read somewhere other than at their desks; they especially like the teacher's desk, a stool, etc. Establish limits for students' voice levels. Have them say their names in "two-inch" (quiet) voices and again in "six-inch" (loud) voices. Tell them to use two-inch (quiet) voices while Partner Reading. Encourage them to coach their partners to allow them to figure out a word rather than just telling them. Remind students that they can use the Guess the Covered Word strategy with their partners. Circulate around the room and coach partners as needed.

AFTER READING

After reading, let students take turns spinning the Story Map Wheel and giving their answers.

WORKING WITH WORDS

MAKING WORDS

In these lessons, you dictate words, and students use small letter cards (or cut apart letter strips) to make these words. (The "secret" word is the last word made and uses all of the letters.) Next, lead students to sort the words for beginning sounds or spelling patterns. The final step is the transfer step. Have students use the sort patterns to decode and spell new words.

MUSEUM VISIT

Making Words Letters: a, a, i, c, f, r, s, t, t ("secret" word: artifacts)

Make: at, cat/act, rat/tar/art, far, car, star, tart, cart, sift, rift, raft, fair, start, craft, stair, Africa, artifacts

Sort: –ar (tar, far, car, star); –art (art, tart, cart, start); –air (fair, stair); –ift (sift, rift); –aft (raft, craft)

Transfer: scar, part, chair, shift, shaft

Making Words Letters: a, i, i g, n, n, p, s, t ("secret" word: paintings)

Make: in, pin, tip, sip, nip, tan, snap, snip, sign/sing, pain, gain, ping, stain, sting, paintings

Sort: –ip (tip, sip, nip, snip); –ing (sing, ping, sting); –ain (pain, gain, stain)

Transfer: strip, swing, plain, drain

Making Words Letters: e, u, u, c, l, p, r, s, s, t ("secret" word: sculptures)

Make: up, sup, cup, pet, set, let, pets/pest, lest, rest, crept, crest, crust, erupt, result, sculpt, culture, sculptures

Sort: –et (pet, set, let); –up (up, sup, cup); –est (pest, lest, rest, crest)

Transfer: jet, pup, west, vest

GUESS THE COVERED WORD

Write the sentences below on an overhead transparency or piece of chart paper. Cover the bold word in each sentence with two, dark colored self-stick notes—one note to cover the "onset" (all of the consonants before the first vowel) and the other note to cover the "rime" (the rest of the word). Let students have four guesses and write these guesses on the transparency or chart paper. Then, uncover the onset. Let students guess again, if necessary. Students will use context clues, beginning letters (onsets), and word length to guess the covered words in these sentences.

GOING ON A FIELD TRIP

1. Our **teacher** took us on a tour through the museum.

2. We saw **paintings** from long ago.

3. We learned about **history** by visiting the museum.

4. My favorite part was the **display** about dinosaurs.

5. My teacher liked the **reptile** exhibit best.

MUSEUM VISIT

WRITING

Tell students a story about an imaginary teacher from an imaginary school who went on a field trip to a nearby museum, but when her students wouldn't behave, she just disappeared. Now, students in her class have a substitute who is meaner than a Tasmanian devil, and they want their old teacher back. Have students design "missing person" posters to hang up around the school just in case somebody in the school might have seen the other teacher. Provide students with photocopied pictures of the "missing person." This could be a picture of a friend or relative who could then actually visit the classroom and pretend she was "found" because of the posters.

Give students some background knowledge about the teacher who is "missing." Allow each student to ask one question and then list your answers on the board. This format gets students involved and thinking like detectives. Students might ask questions, such as:

1. Where was she seen last in the museum?

2. What was she wearing?

3. Has anyone in her family seen her?

4. Has she called anyone?

5. Where does she like to go when she is lonely or upset?

All of these ideas will help students come up with items to add to their posters. Give students copies of real missing person posters so that they can see what is typically found on one. Remind students that each poster needs a phone number in case someone has seen the "missing" teacher. When the posters are complete, post them around the school.

QUICK WRITES OR OTHER IDEAS FOR WRITING MINI-LESSONS

Here are a few Quick Writes that can be posted in the room so that children will have writing activities to work on. These ideas also could be used for other mini-lessons while learning about museums.

- Tell about a time you went to a museum.

- What would you do if you got lost in a museum?

- Write about how you can stay safe in a public place.

FOOD ACTIVITY

DINOSAUR CAKES

INGREDIENTS

- 4 round cakes
- Prepared white frosting
- Cinnamon imperials
- Gumdrops
- Green food coloring

DIRECTIONS

1. Ask a parent to bake four round cakes.

2. Cut each cake in half and then cut one of the halves into pieces as shown below.

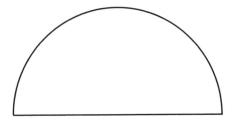 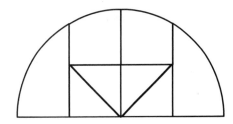

3. Arrange the cut pieces on cookie sheets as shown to create a stegasaurus. Repeat for all four cakes to make one dinosaur cake for each group.

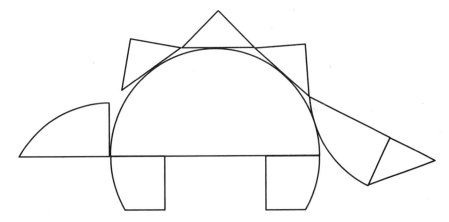

4. Divide the class into four cake-decorating groups. Let the groups decorate their cakes with frosting (add green food coloring to prepared white frosting). Encourage students to use cinnamon imperials for spots and gumdrops for eyes.

Caution: Before completing any food activity, ask families' permission and inquire about students' food allergies and religious or other food preferences.

MUSEUM VISIT

ART ACTIVITY

FOSSIL DIG

Since most students are interested in dinosaurs, this fossil activity will be extremely fun and exciting for them. You will need a box of plaster of paris and some clay. (Check with an art teacher before making any purchases.) Be sure to find out what rules (if any) your school district has for working with plaster of paris and clay. You will also need a container to mix the plaster.

MATERIALS

- Clay
- Plaster of paris
- Small rocks, plastic dinosaurs, seashells, and leaves

DIRECTIONS

1. Tell students to pretend they are paleontologists who have to make fossil molds for a local museum.

2. Give each student a piece of clay. Each student will roll out the clay to a thickness of about 1".

3. Students should select objects they wish to make into fossils and press them into the clay (one object per piece of clay). When each student carefully removes her object, an imprint will be left in the clay.

4. At this point, review how this might have happened in nature.

5. Pour plaster of paris into the clay molds and set them aside to dry. When the molds are dry, students can become paleontologists and "discover" their fossils by removing the plaster of paris from the clay.

CULMINATING ACTIVITY

DINOSAUR PARTY

- Put students' fossils on display and make your room into a mini-museum. Invite other classes, teachers, and administrators to view the fossils.

- Let everyone enjoy the Dinosaur Cakes (page 99).

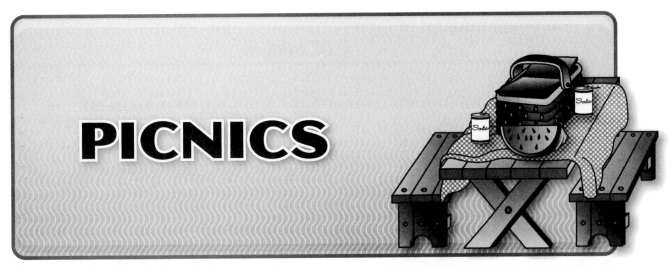

PICNICS

Spring, summer, and fall are great seasons for spending time with family and friends outside, and there's no better way to do it than with a picnic. Whether in a park, at the beach, or in a backyard, picnics are fun. Many fond memories have been made on lazy afternoons in the company of family and friends while eating off paper plates and drinking from plastic cups. Picnics mean eating chicken, sandwiches, potato chips, fruit, and tasty desserts—hopefully without bees and ants. After packing up the picnic basket and picking up the trash, everyone can have fun throwing a football or Frisbee®, playing tag or hide-and-seek, or just enjoying being outside. No matter what kind of food you eat or what sort of activity you do, the key to a great picnic is having fun with your family and friends.

SELF-SELECTED READING

Books for teachers to read aloud and then put in book baskets or on shelves for Self-Selected Reading:

FICTION

The Bears' Picnic by Stan and Jan Berenstain (Random House Books for Young Readers, 1966)
The well-meaning Papa Bear invites his family on a picnic. Unfortunately, finding the right spot to have lunch proves difficult, and the usual near catastrophes occur.

A Picnic in October by Eve Bunting (Voyager Books, 2004)
Tony, a boy of Italian heritage, always has to accompany his grandparents to a "dumb picnic" on Liberty Island in October. He doesn't really understand their enthusiasm until he sees a family of new Americans who have also come to see the statue; only then does he realize what the statue symbolizes.

Picnic by Emily Arnold McCully (HarperCollins, 2003)
Bitty the mouse and her family go on a picnic in their pickup truck. The road is bumpy, and Bitty bounces right off the back of the truck with no one but a stuffed animal to save her. Her parents search frantically for her as soon as they realize she is missing, and they soon find her. Children who have been lost will feel relief similar to Bitty's when she is found.

Let's Go, Froggy! by Jonathan London (Puffin Books, 1996)
Froggy's dad suggests a bicycle day trip and recommends that Froggy bring his bicycle helmet, a butterfly net, a ball, and some other things. Froggy, like many small children, can't

remember where any of his things are. Dad offers the unhelpful hint, "It's where you left it!" Forgetful children (and parents) will recognize themselves in this book.

The Best Picnic Ever by Clare Jarrett (Candlewick Press, 2004)

As Jack and his mother prepare to have a picnic, Jack meets some unlikely playmates: a giraffe, an elephant, a tiger, and more. After a romp in the park, Jack cordially invites his playmates to lunch and enjoys a perfect kid's lunch—hot dogs, pizza, cake, and even strawberries.

Picnic at Mudsock Meadow by Patricia Polacco (Putnam Juvenile, 1992)

Hester loves to pick on William, especially when he is just about to win a contest. At the annual Halloween picnic, he tries to win several of the competitions but never quite succeeds. William may be shy, but he is also brave and resourceful. He decides to jump into the glowing swamp and emerges with a winning Halloween costume and the respect of everyone—even Hester.

We're Going on a Picnic! by Pat Hutchins (Greenwillow, 2002)

It's a beautiful day for a picnic. Hen, Duck, and Goose set out with a basket of delicious food. Each time they stop at a different site, they gather unexpected guests in their basket: a mouse, a squirrel, and even a rabbit. As their basket of food becomes more and more empty, children will laugh more and more.

NONFICTION OR INFORMATIONAL BOOKS

Fireworks, Picnics, and Flags: The Story of the Fourth of July Symbols by James Cross (Clarion Books, 2003)

To celebrate this popular day for picnics, Giblin relates interesting facts of the history of America's Independence Day. The book explores funny anecdotes and explains the meanings of national symbols, such as the Liberty Bell, Uncle Sam, Yankee Doodle, and, of course, the American flag.

Picnic by Chris Baines and Penny Ives (Frances Lincoln, Ltd., 2000)

When two children leave their leftover picnic lunches behind, beetles, butterflies, grubs, and other residents of the woods enjoy a feast. The book demonstrates how humans can impact plants and animals.

Let's Go on a Picnic by Cate Foley (Children's Press, 2001)

This book shows that even busy families can make time for each other. Photographs depict family members as they pack and eat lunch and then play ball. The book includes age-appropriate vocabulary and a glossary.

GUIDED READING

We're Going on a Picnic! by Pat Hutchins (Greenwillow, 2002) is a good choice for Guided Reading in this theme.

PICNICS

BEFORE READING

Bring in a picnic basket with items for a picnic, such as a blanket, plates, spoons, forks, cups, and various types of food (real or toy). Let the children discuss what they would take on a picnic. This would be a good time to introduce or reinforce the U. S. D. A.'s MyPyramid healthy eating plan.

DURING READING (ECHO AND CHORAL READING)

This is easy and repetitive text that could be used for Echo (read after me) or Choral (read with me) Reading. In this particular book, Pat Hutchins tells the story of three animal friends going on a picnic. While they are looking for a perfect spot, other animals take their food out of the basket and eat it. She shows pictures of the animals on previous pages so that children can predict what they think will happen next. They can then read to find out if their predictions are correct. The story also starts at home and ends at home, allowing children to draw a Circle Map (page 123) of where the characters go while searching for the perfect spot.

AFTER READING

Students can reread the story and take turns "doing the book" (acting out the story). Children who do not have action parts can be narrators. In the story, each character brings a favorite food and puts it in the basket. Students can also draw and cut out foods they would take on a picnic. You can collect the drawings in a real basket or a homemade paper one.

WORKING WITH WORDS

MAKING WORDS

In these lessons, you dictate words, and students use small letter cards (or cut apart letter strips) to make these words. (The "secret" word is the last word made and uses all of the letters.) Next, lead students to sort the words for beginning sounds or spelling patterns. The final step is the transfer step. Have students use the sort patterns to decode and spell new words.

Making Words Letters: a, e, b, k, l, n, t ("secret" word: blanket)

Make: an, ban, ant, let, bet, net, bat, tan, ten, take, bake, lake, bank, tank, taken, blank, blanket

Sort: –an (an, ban, tan); –ake (take, bake, lake); –et (let, bet, net, blanket); –ank (bank, tank, blank)

Transfer: fan, flake, wet, rank

Making Words Letters: a, e, i, c, d, h, n, s, s, w ("secret" word: sandwiches)

Make: ad, an, in, win, sin, hid, had, and, die, dies, shin, chin, hand, sand, said, dish, wish, hands, sandwiches

Sort: –in (in, win, sin, shin, chin); –and (and, hand, sand); –ish (dish, wish)

Transfer: fin, land, fish

PICNICS

Making Words Letters: a, e, b, k, s, t
("secret" word: basket)

Make: as, at, eat/ate, bat, sat, tab, bet, set,
stab, sake, bake, take, seat/east, beat, best,
beast, basket

Sort: –at (at, bat, sat); –ab (tab, stab);
–et (bet, set); –ake (sake, bake, take);
–eat (eat, seat, beat); –st (east, best, beast)

Transfer: flat, grab, let, cake, meat, fast

GUESS THE COVERED WORD

Write the sentences below on an overhead transparency or piece of chart paper. Cover the bold word in each sentence with two, dark colored self-stick notes—one note to cover the "onset" (all of the consonants before the first vowel) and the other note to cover the "rime" (the rest of the word). Let students have four guesses and write these guesses on the transparency or chart paper. Then, uncover the onset. Let students guess again, if necessary. Students will use context clues, beginning letters (onsets), and word length to guess the covered words in these sentences.

A PICNIC

1. We are going on a picnic in the **park**.

2. I hope Mom remembers to pack the **drinks**.

3. My sister and I want to eat **chicken** sandwiches.

4. We will eat our food on a **blanket**.

5. My dad wants **chocolate** for dessert.

WRITING

This cooperative writing task allows students to help their peers improve their strengths and work on their weaknesses. In this activity, each student writes the beginning of a story, then reads the beginning and creates the middle of a peer's story, and finally reads another peer's story and develops a conclusion for that story. The pressure of writing an entire story is gone since students are only responsible for parts of three different stories. Although each student will write a beginning, middle, and end, he will not create all three parts of one particular story or idea. Students will work in a collaborative fashion. They might be interested to learn that sometimes authors do not finish stories, and other authors may come back to a writer's idea or story later. An example of this is Dr. Seuss's book *Hooray for Diffendoofer Day* (Knopf Books for Young Readers, 1998). Two authors, Jack Prelutsky and Lane Smith, finished Dr. Seuss's book after he passed away.

Have each student take out a piece of writing paper; students will not write their names on their papers. Next, each student should write the beginning of a story. This should take about 5–10 minutes. When students are finished, have them place their papers on top of the "Beginning of the Story Done" pile and each select a paper from the bottom of the pile. Then, each student has 5–10 minutes to write the middle of his peer's story, building on what happened in the beginning of the story. When students are finished with their "middles," they will put their papers on top of the "Middle of the Story Done" pile and select a paper from the bottom of that pile. Finally, each student has 5–10 minutes to write the ending to his peer's story. Once students are finished, they should keep the stories for which they wrote the endings. They can even illustrate them while they wait for others to finish. This procedure allows slower students to completely finish their thoughts without the pressure to keep up with peers who are more proficient writers.

When you are ready to end the lesson, use a culminating activity that allows each student to read a story to the class. Once each story is read, all of the authors can work together to explain how they thought their stories might end and whether they ended the way they wanted them to. (Remember, no student should ever put his name on any paper, but students should be able to identify the parts of the stories they wrote when they are read aloud.)

For another mini-lesson, model editing using one of the first draft stories. Then, have several students work together to group edit and revise the stories that you assign to them. Using an editor's checklist, they will check for spelling, capitalization, and punctuation mistakes, as well as adding more descriptive language and making sure each sentence is a complete thought. Each group can take their edited version and publish the final draft, either using a word processing program or choosing a group member to copy the final story neatly by hand.

QUICK WRITES OR OTHER IDEAS FOR WRITING MINI-LESSONS

Here are a few Quick Writes that can be posted in the room so that children will have writing activities to work on. These ideas also could be used for other mini-lessons while learning about picnics.

- Tell about a time you went on a picnic.

- What would you pack in your picnic basket?

- Pretend you are an ant at a picnic. How would you get the food?

PICNICS

FOOD (AND SONG) ACTIVITY

ANTS ON A LOG

INGREDIENTS

- Celery stalks
- 1 jar peanut butter
- 1 large box raisins

DIRECTIONS

Wash and cut celery stalks into thirds or fourths. Give each student a paper plate with four cut pieces of celery, 2 tbsp. of peanut butter, and a handful of raisins. Let each student spread peanut butter in the curve of the celery stalks. Have students stick raisins to the peanut butter to create "ants." Sing the song "The Ants Go Marching" and let students act it out after they enjoy their snacks.

Caution: Before completing any food activity, ask families' permission and inquire about students' food allergies and religious or other food preferences.

THE ANTS GO MARCHING

The ants go marching one by one.
Hoorah! Hoorah!
The ants go marching one by one.
Hoorah! Hoorah!
The ants go marching one by one;
The little one stops to suck his thumb,
And they all go marching down into the
ground to get out of the rain.
Boom, boom, boom, boom!

The ants go marching two by two.
Hoorah! Hoorah!
The ants go marching two by two.
Hoorah! Hoorah!
The ants go marching two by two;
The little one stops to tie his shoe,
And they all go marching down into the
ground to get out of the rain.
Boom, boom, boom, boom!

The ants go marching three by three.
Hoorah! Hoorah!
The ants go marching three by three.
Hoorah! Hoorah!
The ants go marching three by three;
The little one stops to climb a tree,
And they all go marching down into the
ground to get out of the rain.
Boom, boom, boom, boom!

The ants go marching four by four.
Hoorah! Hoorah!
The ants go marching four by four.
Hoorah! Hoorah!
The ants go marching four by four;
The little one stops to shut the door,
And they all go marching down into the
ground to get out of the rain.
Boom, boom, boom, boom!

The ants go marching five by five.
Hoorah! Hoorah!
The ants go marching five by five.
Hoorah! Hoorah!
The ants go marching five by five;
The little one stops to take a dive,
And they all go marching down into the
ground to get out of the rain.
Boom, boom, boom, boom!

The ants go marching six by six.
Hoorah! Hoorah!
The ants go marching six by six.
Hoorah! Hoorah!
The ants go marching six by six;
The little one stops to pick up sticks,
And they all go marching down into the
ground to get out of the rain.
Boom, boom, boom, boom!

The ants go marching seven by seven.
Hoorah! Hoorah!
The ants go marching seven by seven.
Hoorah! Hoorah!
The ants go marching seven by seven;
The little one stops to pray to heaven,
And they all go marching down into the
ground to get out of the rain.
Boom, boom, boom, boom!

The ants go marching eight by eight.
Hoorah! Hoorah!
The ants go marching eight by eight.
Hoorah! Hoorah!
The ants go marching eight by eight;
The little one stops to roller-skate,
And they all go marching down into the
ground to get out of the rain.
Boom, boom, boom, boom!

The ants go marching nine by nine.
Hoorah! Hoorah!
The ants go marching nine by nine.
Hoorah! Hoorah!
The ants go marching nine by nine;
The little one stops to check the time,
And they all go marching down into the
ground to get out of the rain.
Boom, boom, boom, boom!

The ants go marching ten by ten.
Hoorah! Hoorah!
The ants go marching ten by ten.
Hoorah! Hoorah!
The ants go marching ten by ten;
The little one stops to shout,
"THE END!"

PICNICS

ART ACTIVITY

PICNIC PLACE MATS

Before starting this activity, make sure students understand the words **over**, **under**, **weave**, **alternate**, and **opposite**. Then, have students do some paper weaving. The finished pieces can be laminated and used for place mats. Let students work on patterns to weave colorful rainbows.

Tip: Ask a volunteer to use a paper cutter to prepare the construction paper strips ahead of time.

MATERIALS

- 1" x 17" strips of colorful construction paper
- 11" x 17" sheets of colorful construction paper
- Rulers
- Pencils
- Glue
- Scissors

DIRECTIONS

1. Let each student fold one piece of construction paper in half, forming a 17" x 5.5" rectangle.

2. Using a ruler and pencil, have each student draw lines 1" apart from the fold to the outer edge. Stop the lines 1" from the edge.

3. Have each student cut along the lines from the fold to the edge. Remind her to stop cutting 1" from the open edge. Then, she should open the paper and place it flat on the table.

4. Demonstrate how to weave the cut strips of paper into the larger piece of paper. Carefully select the colors for your weaving pattern.

5. A drop of glue can be placed at the ends of each weaving strip to hold the pieces in place.

6. Allow the glue to dry and laminate or cover each place mat with clear contact paper.

CULMINATING ACTIVITY

CLASS PICNIC

Invite students to bring bag lunches and towels or blankets to sit on. Then, set up a picnic area outside, eat lunches as a class, and sing, "The Ants Go Marching!" Remind students to bring their Picnic Place Mats.

PLAYING ON A TEAM

Like it or not, sports are a huge part of our culture. Soccer and baseball fields, hockey rinks, and basketball courts are filled with children kicking, swinging, skating, and dribbling. A large number of students play organized sports. Children benefit from playing team sports as long as they are having fun. And, research shows that students who participate in sports often do better academically and are more organized.

Team sports can add to a child's sense of identity because he can say, "I'm a Little Leaguer," or, "I play tee ball." Team sports also provide children with an opportunity to develop their physical skills and, as they actually master the skills, to develop self-confidence. Besides the physical benefits, sports help children learn to socialize and cooperate. Sports also allow students to interact with other children and adults in an environment that is different from school.

Since not all students play team sports, it is important to expose them to these activities at school and allow them opportunities to listen as other children share their experiences with different kinds of sports. There are numerous books about sports, the challenges of being on a team, and learning to be a team player. By allowing children to live vicariously through stories, you will better prepare them for how to act when they win, lose, or don't get to play the whole game.

SELF-SELECTED READING

Books for teachers to read aloud and then put in book baskets or on shelves for Self-Selected Reading:

FICTION

Young Cam Jansen and the Baseball Mystery by David A. Adler (Puffin Books, 2001)
Cam Jansen puts her photographic memory to use when a much-needed baseball disappears in the park. Cam, her friend Eric, and a group of helpful kids get together to solve the mystery.

Cam Jansen and the Mystery of the Babe Ruth Baseball by David A. Adler (Puffin Books, 2004)
Enjoy more adventures of Cam Jansen and her friend Eric as they try to solve the mystery of a missing baseball signed by the Babe himself.

Soccer Sam by Jean Marzollo (Random House Books for Young Readers, 1987)
Sam can't wait for his cousin Marco to visit from Mexico. Unfortunately, Sam's excitement turns into embarrassment when Marco seems more interested in hitting a basketball with his head. Sam's opinion changes when Marco teaches Sam and the other second graders to play soccer. Their new soccer skills wow even the big third graders when the two groups meet in a soccer match.

Max by Rachel Isadora (Aladdin Paperbacks, 1984)
Max plays baseball every Saturday while his sister takes ballet. As a dedicated baseball player, Max will go to any lengths to improve his skills, including adopting some of the warm-up moves from his sister's ballet class.

Not Just Tutus by Rachel Isadora (Putnam Juvenile, 2003)
This funny collection of poems captures the graceful triumphs of ballet dancing as well as the occasional not-so-graceful mishap. Both boys and girls are depicted learning to dance.

Ronald Morgan Goes to Bat by Patricia Reilly Giff (Puffin Books, 1990)
Parents and children who have struggled together through the beginning stages of learning a sport will enjoy this tale of perseverance. Ronald's awkwardness at baseball is only equaled by his enthusiasm for the game. Once Ronald learns to keep his eye on the ball, he begins to improve.

Three Cheers for Tacky by Helen Lester (Houghton Mifflin Company, 1996)
Tacky the Penguin and his friends are determined to win the Penguin Cheering Contest. Tacky doesn't exactly do a perfect job, but the judges award him points for his entertainment value and originality.

Clifford's Sports Day by Norman Bridwell (Cartwheel, 1996)
Clifford joins Emily Elizabeth and her friends at school for a day of outdoor games. He uses sack race bags as booties, makes a mess of the hurdles, and lends his size to the tug of war competition.

NONFICTION OR INFORMATIONAL BOOKS

Our Soccer League by Chuck Solomon, (Knopf Books for Young Readers, 1988) Two Brooklyn soccer teams, the Sluggers and the Falcons, are depicted as they compete in league matches. Color photographs show readers the excitement of the young players.

Our Little League by Chuck Solomon (Knopf Books for Young Readers, 1988) Watch the Little Mets as they practice and then play the Bombers. Children will appreciate this beautifully photographed and lighthearted introduction to baseball.

The Everything Kids Baseball Book: Star Players, Great Teams, Baseball Legends, and Tips on Playing Like a Pro by Richard Mintzer (Adams Media Corporation, 2004) Fans and players alike will love this book that explores all aspects of baseball from playing to statistics to card collecting.

GUIDED READING

Here Comes the Strikeout! by Leonard Kessler (HarperTrophy, 1992) is a delightful book that works well for Guided Reading.

DAY 1
BEFORE READING (VOCABULARY)

Cut out ten paper baseballs and ten paper baseball mitts. Write each of the following words on a baseball:

- slump
- strikeouts
- tapped
- helmets
- choose

- shortstop
- inning
- laughed
- yelled
- glove

Write the definition for each word on a paper mitt. Let students match the baseballs to the correct mitts.

Then, have students predict what the story will be about based on these words. (In this story, the main character has a hard time hitting the ball.) Let students tell if they have trouble with sports or how they could help others who do. As a further connection, play a game of baseball or kickball during recess.

DURING READING

Divide the class into "teams" of four or five students and have the best reader in each group be the "coach." Have students read the story together in these Play School Groups or "reading teams."

AFTER READING

Have students remain in their groups. Have each group complete a Story Map (page 90) to present to the class.

PLAYING ON A TEAM

DAY 2

BEFORE READING

Review the story using the Story Map.

DURING READING

Have students reread the story independently and silently to find their favorite parts.

AFTER READING

Have students discuss with their groups or as a class which parts of this story they liked best.

WORKING WITH WORDS

MAKING WORDS

In these lessons, you dictate words, and students use small letter cards (or cut apart letter strips) to make these words. (The "secret" word is the last word made and uses all of the letters.) Next, lead students to sort the words for beginning sounds or spelling patterns. The final step is the transfer step. Have students use the sort patterns to decode and spell new words.

Making Words Letters: a, e, o, k, m, r, t, w ("secret" word: teamwork)

Make: to, tow, mow, row, tea/eat/ate, rate, mate/meat/team, work, wake, take, make, mark, maker, taker, teamwork

Sort: –ate (ate, mate, rate); –ake (take, make, wake); –ow (tow, mow, row)

Transfer: state, brake, bow

Making Words Letters: i, o, u, f, m, n, r, s ("secret" word: uniforms)

Make: is, us, sun, run, fun, son, for, four, from, firm, form, norm/morn, uniforms

Sort: –un (run, sun, fun); –orm (form, norm); homonyms (sun, son; for, four)

Transfer: bun, stun, dorm, storm

Making Words Letters: a, e, y, l, p, r, s ("secret" word: players)

Make: as, say, pay, lay, yes, ear, sea, sale, seal, real, yelp, play, slay, year, spry, plea, reply, replay/player, players

Sort: –ay (say, lay, pay, play, slay); –ear (ear, year); –eal (real, seal); re– (reply, replay)

Transfer: stay, clay, near, steal, retry

PLAYING ON A TEAM

GUESS THE COVERED WORD

Write the sentences below on an overhead transparency or piece of chart paper. Cover the bold word in each sentence with two, dark colored self-stick notes—one note to cover the "onset" (all of the consonants before the first vowel) and the other note to cover the "rime" (the rest of the word). Let students have four guesses and write these guesses on the transparency or chart paper. Then, uncover the onset. Let students guess again, if necessary. Students will use context clues, beginning letters (onsets), and word length to guess the covered words in these sentences.

TEAM PLAYERS

1. I am on a **soccer** team.

2. We cheer for our **teammates.**

3. Our team needs to **practice** to do well.

4. The players need to **kick** the ball into the goal to score a point.

5. The **crowd** cheers for us!

WRITING

The basis of this activity is sequencing sentences by using sentence strips like puzzle pieces. Each group of three or four students will have all of the sentences written for a personal narrative. However, the sentences will not be in order. Students will use their knowledge of good writing to help put the story together. If students do not have a good understanding of the structure of a personal narrative—that it has an introduction, supporting sentences with detail sentences, and a closing—spend some time discussing the structure before introducing this lesson.

First, write the word **teamwork** on the board. Then, use a Circle Map (page 123) to list all of the words that relate to teamwork. This will help those students with little or no experience of being on a team build some background knowledge. It will also help other students activate their prior knowledge. Once there are several ideas on the Circle Map, add any other important words that may have been overlooked and need to be emphasized for the lesson.

SAMPLE PERSONAL NARRATIVE

Ahead of time, write a mini-lesson about team sports. Stress the sequence of what happens and how it feels to play on a team. Here is an example:

I love to play team sports. I play on a soccer team called the Dragons. I am the goalie for my team. My job is to keep the ball from getting into the goal. When I stop a ball, I must throw or kick it back onto the field. I throw or kick it as hard as

113

I can. Sometimes, I talk to the other players on my team. I tell them to get the ball and to kick it away. I love to be on a team. I hope that I can play soccer every spring and fall.

For the lesson, copy your personal narrative onto sentence strips—one sentence per strip. Make enough copies for all of your groups to have the complete narrative. Mix up each set of sentence strips and give one set to each group.

Wander around the room making sure all of the students have put the story into the correct sequence. Ask them how it feels to work together as a team.

QUICK WRITES OR OTHER IDEAS FOR WRITING MINI-LESSONS:

Here are a few Quick Writes that can be posted in the room so that children will have writing activities to work on. These ideas also could be used for other mini-lessons while learning about playing on a team.

- Tell about a favorite sport.

- Make up a new game and be sure to list the rules.

- Research a famous athlete and write about some interesting facts that you learn.

ART ACTIVITY

BASEBALL PAPERWEIGHTS

Shape homemade play dough into "baseballs." After they dry, let students paint them white with red "stitches."

MATERIALS

- 2 cups flour
- 1 cup water
- 1 cup salt
- White and red tempera paint

DIRECTIONS

1. Have students help you mix all of the ingredients together.

2. Let students knead the dough on a floured surface, adding additional flour if the mixture is too sticky or more water if it is too dry.

3. Let students roll the dough into ball shapes.

4. Let the balls air dry or bake them in a 250° F oven for about 1½ hours or until the dough is hard to the touch. Cool on a wire rack.

5. When the baseballs are cool, let students paint them white and then add the red "stitches."

CULMINATING ACTIVITY

SPORTS DAY

- Let students wear uniforms from sports they play or like to watch.

- Make a nutritious snack using teamwork. Have students bring different fresh or canned fruits. Mix them together to make a fruit salad. Serve with a sports drink. Let students eat the special "Teamwork Salad" and write about their favorite sports.

  Caution: Before completing any food activity, ask families' permission and inquire about students' food allergies and religious or other food preferences.

- Show students the importance of being kind to others and getting along. Hold an unpeeled banana and instruct each student to say something mean like, "I don't like you," or, "You can't catch very well." Each time a student says something unkind, gently squeeze the banana. After every child has had a turn, slowly peel the banana (for effect). Students will see a very bruised banana. Explain that people also get hurt on the inside when they are treated poorly. Make a chart of kind and encouraging things to say to others or ways to show good sportsmanship.

RAIN

What is weather? In many parts of the world, some days are nice and sunny, some days are cold and cloudy, and some days are rainy and damp. Many children live where there is a variety of weather depending on the time of year. If your students experience four seasons, then they usually have at least some rain during all of the four seasons. Other children live in deserts where it seldom rains. Children who live in deserts know little about rain, walking in puddles, thunderstorms, and floods. Students can have fun in the rain, but rainy weather can also bring problems.

A rainy day often makes students feel lazy. They can't play or work outside or go to the park. Students often feel that there is "nothing to do" because they would rather be outside than stay inside. For young children (and older people), rainy days can be great reading days. There is nothing quite so enjoyable as curling up with a good book on a rainy day and reading.

SELF-SELECTED READING

Books for teachers to read aloud and then put in book baskets or on shelves for Self-Selected Reading:

FICTION

The Rain Came Down by David Shannon (Blue Sky Press, 2000)
As the rain pours down on a community, its members reflect the mood of the rain by squabbling. Fortunately, the sun comes out, a rainbow appears, and everyone is all smiles again.

Splish, Splash, Spring by Jan Carr (Holiday House, 2002)
Rhyming text tells the story of three children and their dog as they enjoy the rain. The usual signs of spring—robins, worms, blooming bulbs, and a thundershower—are part of the day's fun.

Bringing the Rain to Kapiti Plain by Verne Aardema (Puffin Books, 1992)
In this rhyming African tale, a little boy must help his sick father bring much-needed rain to the drought-stricken Kapiti Plain.

Listen to the Rain by Bill Martin and John Archambault (Henry Holt and Company, 1988)
This tried-and-true writing team creates a beautifully written exploration of the different phases of a rain shower. Striking and unusual illustrations accompany the text.

Amazing Rain by Sam Brown (Soft Skull Press, 2004)
A graphic novelist uses brightly colored drawings to tell a fable about rain in the city.

Rain Romp: Stomping Away a Grouchy Day by Jane Kurtz (Greenwillow Books, 2002)
A little rain is no reason to have a bad day. A girl and her parents splash around and then return home to also enjoy some indoor fun.

Come On, Rain by Karen Hesse (Scholastic Press, 1999)
Rain in the city can be just as refreshing as rain in the country. Tess celebrates as her wish for rain is realized.

NONFICTION OR INFORMATIONAL BOOKS

Down Comes the Rain by Franklyn M. Branley (HarperTrophy, 1997)
Teachers and parents alike can use this informative and engaging book to explore the water cycle, including details about how clouds, rain, and hail are formed. Readers can also complete a few science activities.

Where Does the Water Go? by Mario Lucca (National Geographic Society, 2001)
This text explains three common situations in which the process of evaporation occurs: in the sun, in a clothes dryer, and on a stove top.

The Rain Forest by Pat Malone (National Geographic Society, 2001)
Malone's book goes beyond rain to a diverse ecosystem that is made possible by a consistent amount of rain. Four vertical levels of the rain forest are examined.

Desert Rain by Pat Malone (National Geographic Society, 2001)
When the rains finally come to the dry desert, they transform a seemingly barren place into a completely different landscape.

Rain by Robert Kalan (HarperTrophy, 1991)
Simple text introduces even very young readers to the colors and sounds of rainy weather.

Rain by Manya Stojic (Crown Books for Young Readers, 2000)
African animals use their senses to track an approaching storm.

GUIDED READING

Bringing the Rain to Kapiti Plain by Verna Aardema (Puffin Books, 1992) is a story that students need to hear before they read it. First, students need to listen and hear the rhythm and the repetition in the story. Then, students need to look at the pictures and talk about the story—what is happening—before they try to read it.

DAY 1
BEFORE READING

Read the book aloud and have students listen to the rhythm and rhymes. Then, tell them they will have an opportunity to read the book themselves. But first, take a Picture Walk with students through the book, looking at the pictures and vocabulary and talking about what is happening in the book.

RAIN

VOCABULARY

Introduce the following words with Rivet (page 26):

- acacia trees
- creatures
- giraffes
- browse
- pasture
- belated
- migrated
- drought
- shadowed
- eagle
- feature
- pierced
- thunder

DURING READING (ECHO AND CHORAL READING)

Let students Echo Read—reading after you—as you read this story. Once it repeats, tell students that they can join in and Choral Read the repeating lines with you. Or, you can assign lines to students and have them join in each time their lines repeat.

AFTER READING (DRAW AFTER READING)

Let students illustrate their favorite lines or favorite page. When students finish, have them form a circle, show their drawings, and share their favorite parts.

WORKING WITH WORDS

MAKING WORDS

In these lessons, you dictate words, and students use small letter cards (or cut apart letter strips) to make these words. (The "secret" word is the last word made and uses all of the letters.) Next, lead students to sort the words for beginning sounds or spelling patterns. The final step is the transfer step. Have students use the sort patterns to decode and spell new words.

Making Words Letters: a, a, i, f, l, l, n, r ("secret" word: rainfall)

Make: in, an, ran, fan, far, air, fair, fail, rail, rain, frail/flair, final, rainfall

Sort: –an (an, ran, fan); –air (air, fair, flair); –ail (fail, rail, frail)

Transfer: plan, chair, stair, trail

Making Words Letters: a, i, o, b, n, r, w ("secret" word: rainbow)

Make: on, an, ran, row, bow, war, warn, barn, rain, brain, brown, robin, rainbow

Sort: –an (an, ran); –ow (row, bow); –ain (rain, brain)

Transfer: scan, glow, flow, drain

Making Words Letters: e, o, u, d, h, m, n, r, r, s, s, t, t ("secret" word: thunderstorms)

Make: do, due, Sue, true, storms, south, north, detour, students, monsters, thunder, southern, thunderstorms

Sort: –ue (due, Sue, true); plurals (storms, students, monsters, thunderstorms)

Transfer: flue, glue, detours

118

© CARSON-DELLOSA • INTEGRATING READING, WRITING, AND WORDS LESSONS • CD-104194

RAIN

ROUNDING UP THE RHYMES

Splish, Splash, Spring by Jan Carr (Holiday House, 2002) is a rhyming book about spring—
puddles, **birds**, **sunshine**, **kites**, and **rain**!

Read the book aloud and let students enjoy the rhymes and pictures. Then, read it again and have students listen for the rhymes and "round them up." Write the rhyming pairs on a board or on index cards that will be displayed in a pocket chart.

sloppy	seeking	cheeping
raindroppy	peeking	peeping
pocus	frilly, silly	raindrops
crocus	daffodilly	drops
	willy-nilly	
swooping	whipping	blooming
looping	slipping	perfumy

Next, call attention to the spelling patterns (how these rhymes are written). Get rid of any sets that do not have the same spelling pattern. This book only has one set of rhymes with different patterns.

sloppy	seeking	cheeping
raindroppy	peeking	peeping
pocus	frilly, silly	raindrops
crocus	daffodilly	drops
	willy-nilly	
swooping	whipping	~~blooming~~
looping	slipping	~~perfumy~~

Finally, use these spelling patterns to read and write transfer words.

READING TRANSFER

Show students the following words, one at a time, written on separate index cards: **sleeping** and **creeping**. Show the words to students; don't say them. For each word, ask students, "What if I were reading and came to this word? Which words on the board would help me read it?" If students can't read the words on the index cards, hold each card under the words with the same pattern and read down (for example, **cheeping**, **peeping**, **sleeping**, **creeping**).

WRITING TRANSFER

Ask students, "What if it was writing time and I wanted to write **drooping**? The flowers in the backyard were **drooping**. Which words on the board would help me write **drooping**? Yes, l-o-o-p-i-n-g and s-w-o-o-p-i-n-g." Write **drooping** on an index card or the board. Have students spell the word as you say it. If students can't spell the word, then put the blank index card under the words with the same pattern and stretch out the **d-r** as you write it. Then, finish the word with the pattern **–ooping**.

RAIN

GUESS THE COVERED WORD

Write the sentences below on an overhead transparency or piece of chart paper. (Write the name of a student on each line. This makes the activity even more fun!) Cover the bold word in each sentence with two, dark colored self-stick notes—one note to cover the "onset" (all of the consonants before the first vowel) and the other note to cover the "rime" (the rest of the word). Let students have four guesses and write these guesses on the transparency or chart paper. Then, uncover the onset. Let students guess again, if necessary. Students will use context clues, beginning letters (onsets), and word length to guess the covered words in these sentences.

WHEN IT RAINS

1. _____ likes to walk in **puddles**.

2. _____ sees **clouds** in the sky.

3. _____ looks out the window and sees **raindrops**.

4. _____ is sad; he can't **play** outside.

5. _____ likes to wear a blue **raincoat**.

WRITING

POETRY

Writing poetry can be fun! Try writing a cinquain with your students. A cinquain usually consists of five unrhymed lines that are made up of two, four, six, eight, and two syllables. Or, try writing a simplified variation with lines of one word, two words, three words, four words, and one word.

In your mini-lesson, model a simple variation of a cinquain like this one:

Rain

falling down

on my umbrella,

my head, and jacket

wet!

QUICK WRITES OR OTHER IDEAS FOR WRITING MINI-LESSONS:

Here are a few Quick Writes that can be posted in the room so that children will have writing activities to work on. These ideas also could be used for other mini-lessons while learning about rain.

- Summarize the story *Bringing the Rain to Kapiti Plain*.

- Write an informational piece about rain.

- Write about a rainy day in your life.

RAIN

ART ACTIVITY

RAINY DAY COLLAGES

MATERIALS

- Scissors
- Colorful construction paper
- Glue sticks

Model how to make a collage. Use a large piece of light blue construction paper for the background. Cut or tear green construction paper to make grass and glue it in place. Combine brown and green paper to make a tree. Make a house that looks like your house. Finally, make a child wearing a rain hat, raincoat, and boots and holding a colorful umbrella. After you are finished, let students make their own rainy day collages.

CULMINATING ACTIVITY

RAINY DAY PARTY

- Let students bring rain boots, rubber shoes, raincoats, plastic ponchos, and umbrellas to school. Remember to discuss rules about having umbrellas inside!

- Dress in rain gear. Then, read a rainy day book aloud or pretend you are reading in the rain.

- Let students play inside games that would be good on a rainy day. Have fun!

SLEEPING OVER

Summertime and weekends are perfect opportunities to unroll sleeping bags for sleepovers. Despite their popularity, sleepovers can sometimes be challenging and overwhelming for children because they may be nervous about missing Mom and Dad, scared of the dark, or afraid of wetting the bed. Sleepovers are rites of passage for children and they can be great fun. Since most children have stayed overnight at a friend's or relative's house, they can build on their own experiences. For those children who have yet to experience a sleepover, reading and writing about sleeping over can ease their fears about this activity.

SELF-SELECTED READING

Books for teachers to read aloud and then put in book baskets or on shelves for Self-Selected Reading:

FICTION

Amanda Pig and Her Best Friend Lollipop
by Jean Van Leeuwen (Puffin, 2000)
Amanda Pig and her friend Lollipop decide to have their very first sleepover party at Lollipop's house. Amanda experiences the typical nerves that are part of sleeping away from home for the first time.

Arthur's First Sleepover by Marc Brown
(Little, Brown and Company, 1996)
Arthur and his friends decide to have a sleepover, despite rumors about alien sightings.

Messy Bessey and the Birthday Overnight
by Patricia and Fredrick McKissack (Children's Press, 1999)
Messy Bessey and her friends enjoy a wild time at a birthday sleepover, but Bessey stays to help clean up the mess.

Edward's Overwhelming Overnight by Rosemary Wells (Dial Books for Young Readers, 1995)
The unusual plot of this book has Edward attempting to stay overnight at his friend's house during a snowstorm. However, he just isn't ready for it. The message is that it's OK to be not quite ready yet.

The Case of the Spooky Sleepover by James Preller (Scholastic Paperbacks, 2001) Ralphie Jordan thinks his house is haunted, and Jigsaw Jones is on the case. The junior sleuth spends the night and helps piece together all of the ghostly clues.

Iris and Walter: The Sleepover by Elissa Haden Guest (Gulliver Books Paperbacks, 2003) Iris cannot wait for her first sleepover at her best friend Walter's house. She looks forward to having a puppet show, riding Walter's horse, and more. She has a wonderful time until bedtime when she becomes unbearably homesick, so Walter and his family willingly drive her home.

NONFICTION OR INFORMATIONAL BOOKS

Creative Sleepovers for Kids! Fun Activities, Themes, and Ideas for Overnight Parties for Boys or Girls by Julie Kauffman (Prima Lifestyles, 2002) Boys, girls, and parents will love the sleepover themes, invitation and decoration ideas, and fun games included in this book.

Let's Have a Slumber Party (Barnes & Noble Books, 2002) This book provides fun, innovative tips to prevent party problems and make sure participants have a great time.

Sleeping Over by Melinda Beth Radabaugh (Heinemann Library, 2002) Color photographs explain where, how, and why a sleepover can take place as they instruct first-timers about what to bring and what to expect.

The Sleepover Journal: A Light-Pen Diary by Jon Kauffman (Chronicle Books, 2002) Kauffman's book doubles as a party planner and a fill-in journal. Included are recipes, games, and group activities, as well as a guest book for friends to fill out.

GUIDED READING

Arthur's First Sleepover by Marc Brown (Little, Brown and Company, 1996) works well for second and third grades.

DAY 1
BEFORE READING

Create a circle map with the word **sleepover** in the middle. Ask students to tell you what they think of when they hear the word. Write what students say in the area around the middle circle.

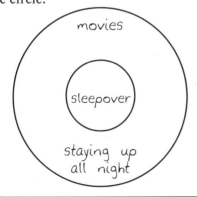

VOCABULARY

Introduce the following vocabulary with Rivet (page 26):

- communicate
- unfamiliar
- flashlight
- breathing
- flaps
- noticed
- crept
- aliens

Then, write the words on one side of the board (chart paper, overhead transparency, etc.) and the definitions in a different order on the other side. Have students match the definitions to the words.

SLEEPING OVER

DURING READING (PARTNER READING)

Divide the class into "chair" partners. Instruct partners to put their chairs back to back. For many classes this will minimize the noise level during Partner Reading.

AFTER READING

Have students discuss the story with their partners after reading. Then, bring the whole class together to discuss and summarize the story.

DAY 2
BEFORE READING

Review the story summary.

DURING READING

Have students reread the book as a whole group, with partners, or in Three-Ring Circus (page 11). It can be your choice or let the class choose.

AFTER READING

Have each student fold a letter-sized piece of paper the long, "hot-dog" way first and then fold it the wide, "hamburger" way two times. This will create eight squares. Students will use the folded papers as graphic organizers. In the top left square, have students write **Title and Author**. Proceeding to the right, then continuing left to right down the page, have students fill in the remaining seven squares with the following words: **Character**, **Setting**, **Problem**, **Author's Purpose**, **Conclusion**, **Events**, and **Solution**. Then, instruct students to write and/or draw the answers. (Drawing makes the activity more multilevel.) Have students share their answers with the class, their groups, or their partners, depending on the chosen format.

WORKING WITH WORDS

MAKING WORDS

In these lessons, you dictate words, and students use small letter cards (or cut apart letter strips) to make these words. (The "secret" word is the last word made and uses all of the letters.) Next, lead students to sort the words for beginning sounds or spelling patterns. The final step is the transfer step. Have students use the sort patterns to decode and spell new words.

Making Words Letters: a, a, a, j, m, p, s ("secret" word: pajamas)

Make: as, am, jam, Pam/map, sap/spa, Spam®/maps, pajamas

Sort: –am (am, jam, Pam, Spam); –ap (map, sap)

Transfer: cram, scram, trap, snap

Making Words Letters: a, i, f, g, h, h, l, l, s, t ("secret" word: flashlight)

Make: as, has, his, gas/sag, tag, all, hall, fall, tall, fast, fist, lash, gash/shag, stall, flash, light, sight, fight, slight, flashlight

Sort: –ag (tag, sag, shag); –all (all, tall, hall, fall, stall); –ight (sight, fight, light, slight, flashlight)

Transfer: drag, small, night

SLEEPING OVER

Making Words Letters: i, o, l, l, p, s, w
("secret" word: pillows)

Make: so, sop, sip, lip, low, sow, slow, slop,
slip, pill, sill, will, lips, pills, pillows

Sort: –ip (sip, lip, slip); –ill (will, pill, sill);
–ow (low, sow, slow)

Transfer: ship, still, blow, snow

GUESS THE COVERED WORD

Write the sentences below on an overhead transparency or piece of chart paper. Cover the bold word in each sentence with two, dark colored self-stick notes—one note to cover the "onset" (all of the consonants before the first vowel) and the other note to cover the "rime" (the rest of the word). Let students have four guesses and write these guesses on the transparency or chart paper. Then, uncover the onset. Let students guess again, if necessary. Students will use context clues, beginning letters (onsets), and word length to guess the covered words in these sentences.

AT MY SLEEPOVER

1. We are going to eat **pizza** at my sleepover.

2. We are going to tell **jokes**.

3. I hope there is enough time to watch **movies**.

4. My mother always likes to tell **scary** stories.

5. Sleepovers always make me feel **happy**.

WRITING

This writing mini-lesson focuses on sequencing while further developing students' personal narrative writing skills. Set the scene for this writing activity using art. Talk about something that happens at a sleepover (for example, eating pizza) and then sketch it for students.

Ask each student to draw (but not label) one activity that he might do at a sleepover. In order to make all of the pictures work together, tell students to imagine there are only two people at this sleepover: the student artist and one other person. If the artist is a boy, there will be two boys, and if the artist is a girl, there will be two girls. The picture could be something as simple as two friends eating popcorn or playing a board game. (If you have students who have never been to a sleepover, read a book during a preceding teacher read-aloud that will provide them with some ideas for sleepover activities they would like to draw.)

After students have finished, collect their drawings and put them in two different piles: girls and boys. Randomly, select four drawings from one stack and have students decide if the activities depicted would have to happen in a particular order. After discussing sequencing with students, brainstorm a list of words that show order (for example, **first**, **second**, **next**, **then**, **finally**, etc.). As students become more proficient with sequencing, you can move from single words to phrases to help transition a story.

After you have selected and displayed several sets of four drawings from both piles, ask each student to pick one of the sets to write a story about. The goal is to write a story that talks about the different things happening in each of the drawings. Since there are four drawings, there should be an introductory sentence, two or three other sentences with transition words, and a conclusion. If students are more advanced, they should add sentences that include details about each of the sentences with transition words.

For beginning writers, you might model a simple piece like this:

I had a sleepover at my friend Jill's house. First, we watched movies. After that, we ate ice cream. Then, her mom painted our nails. Finally, we colored pictures. I had a lot of fun at that sleepover.

For more advanced second- and third-grade writers, you might write:

I had a sleepover at my best friend Jill's house on Saturday. First, we watched a scary movie. There were a lot of ghosts and monsters in the movie. After that, we ate chocolate ice cream with sprinkles. I added nuts to mine because I love the way they crunch. Then, her mom painted our fingernails pink. I asked her to do my toes, but she was too tired. Finally, we colored pictures of our favorite teachers. I colored a picture of my second-grade teacher. I had a lot of fun at that sleepover. I hope my mom will let me have Jill over next week.

After students finish writing their stories, have the class come back together and let several students share their stories. Leave the sequenced drawings on display while students are reading. Point to each picture as it happens in the story to monitor whether the story is following the same sequence as the pictures.

QUICK WRITES OR OTHER IDEAS FOR WRITING MINI-LESSONS

Here are a few Quick Writes that can be posted in the room so that children will have writing activities to work on. These ideas also could be used for other mini-lessons while learning about sleepovers.

- Some people like to tell ghost stories at sleepovers. Write a ghost story.

- Write about a time you went to a sleepover or had one at your house.

- Describe your favorite sleepover activity or food.

SLEEPING OVER

FOOD ACTIVITY

MINI-PIZZAS

INGREDIENTS

- Canned refrigerator biscuits
- Can or jar of pizza sauce
- Shredded mozzarella
- Pizza toppings
- Aluminum foil

Give each student a piece of aluminum foil with her name written on it. Divide the uncooked biscuits so that each child has a biscuit. Let students flatten the dough into small pizza crusts on the pieces of foil and add pizza sauce, toppings, and shredded mozzarella. Cook the pizzas according to the instructions on the biscuit can.

Caution: Before completing any food activity, ask families' permission and inquire about students' food allergies and religious or other food preferences.

ART ACTIVITY

TELESCOPES

MATERIALS

- Markers or crayons
- Paper towel tubes
- Black construction paper
- Straight pins
- Glue

Have students bring in paper towels tubes and let them decorate their tubes with markers or crayons. Help each student cover one end of his tube with a piece of black construction paper and glue it into place. Use a straight pin to poke holes through the black paper. When students look through the open ends of the tubes, the pinholes will shine like stars in the night sky.

CULMINATING ACTIVITY

PAJAMA DAY

- Let students wear their pajamas and eat popcorn and the Mini-Pizzas. Students can also read books while lying in their sleeping bags.

- Play flashlight tag in the dark. (Allow some light in to keep the room from being too dark.) Have one student be "It." This student scans the room using a flashlight. The other students crawl around on the floor to avoid being "tagged" by the light.

SNOW

In winter, it snows—that is, it snows if you live in the northern part of the United States or Canada. If you and your students live in the southern part of the United States, in the deserts of California and Arizona, in Mexico, or in Central or South America, then your students (and maybe you and the other teachers in your school) know little about snow or may have never even seen it. Reading and learning about snow is fascinating to many students. Waking up one morning to freshly fallen snow is a magical event, even for people who are accustomed to seeing snow! Wondering what snow really looks and feels like is not unusual for students who have not experienced snow. If you can't take students on a field trip to a snowy place (and most teachers can't), then you can read and learn about this cold, wonderful weather.

SELF-SELECTED READING

Books for teachers to read aloud and then put in book baskets or on shelves for Self-Selected Reading:

FICTION

The Snowy Day by Ezra Jack Keats (Puffin Books, 1976)
Peter wakes up to a perfect, snowy day. Sparse text and beautiful illustrations capture the joy of a child as he plays in the snow.

The First Snowfall by Anne and Harlow Rockwell (Aladdin, 1992)
A young girl watches the snow fall one night, then gets up and goes outside to join the snowplows, skiers, shovelers, and everyone else who is enjoying the snow.

Snow Dance by Lezlie Evans (Houghton Mifflin Company, 1997)
Follow rhyming text to find out what wonders a snow dance may bring.

Here Comes the Snow by Angela Shelf Medearis (Cartwheel, 1996)
Very simple yet appealing text captures the anticipation and then enjoyment of a snowfall.

The Snow Bear by Miriam Moss (Dutton Juvenile, 2000)
When a polar bear cub loses his mother, his animal friends help him build a snowy companion to snuggle with until his mother finds him the next morning.

Stella, Queen of the Snow by Marie-Louise Gay (Scholastic, Inc., 2000)
Stella takes her little brother Sam outside and shares all that she knows about snow in typical "big sister" fashion.

Snow Day! by Patricia Lakin (Dial, 2002)
Crocodiles Sam and Pam and Will and Jill decide to pose as school principals and declare a snow day, much to the delight of their snow-loving friends.

The Biggest Snowball Fight! by Angela Shelf Medearis (Scholastic, Inc, 2003)
In this easy-to-read rhyming book, readers learn the story of a snowball fight.

NONFICTION OR INFORMATIONAL BOOKS

Snow Is Falling by Franklyn M. Branley (HarperTrophy, 2000)
Even very young readers will learn the science of snow in this simple text. Eventually, Branley moves from scientific facts to observations about how people can enjoy snow and the problems snow can cause.

Footprints in the Snow by Cynthia Benjamin (Cartwheel, 1994)
Many different animals make their way through this simply written, informational book, leaving their footprints behind in the snow.

Winter Visitors by Elizabeth Lee O'Donnell (HarperCollins Publishers, 1997)
This counting book tells the story of different groups of animals that decide to drop in at the home of a little girl. The appearance of a skunk in the kitchen, who does what skunks do, gives the opportunity for the animal count to go in reverse.

GUIDED READING: FICTION

Here Comes the Snow by Angela Shelf Medearis (Cartwheel, 1996) is an easy-to-read book. You could also use *The First Snowfall* by Anne and Harlow Rockwell (Aladdin, 1992), *The Snowy Day* by Ezra Jack Keats (Puffin Books, 1976), or any book with a simple sentence on each page. *The Biggest Snowball Fight!* by Angela Shelf Medearis (Scholastic, Inc., 2003) is a book that could be read by many first graders and easily read by most second-grade students.

DAY 1
BEFORE READING

Take a picture walk through the book with your students. Talk about what is happening on each page. Ask students, "What do you think the story will be about?" (predicting).

DURING
(ECHO READING)

Have students Echo Read. Read the text on each page aloud. Then, have students become the echo and read the same text after you.

AFTER READING

Talk about what happens in the story. Were students' predictions correct? If students have had any experiences with snow, ask them if what happened in the book has ever happened to them (text-to-self connections).

If there is time the same day or on the following day, have your students read this story again—by themselves.

DAY 2
BEFORE READING

Build background knowledge by talking about rhyming words and snowballs. You might share if you have ever made a snowball, if you have ever taken part in a snowball fight, or any "snowball stories" you have (text-to-self connections).

DURING READING (INDEPENDENT OR PARTNER READING)

Have children read aloud (whisper reading) with partners or read silently by themselves to find out who (characters), where (setting), when (setting), what happened (event #1), and how the story ended (conclusion) and why.

AFTER READING

Discuss the story—who, what, where, when, why, and how. Use a winter glove (one finger for each W and the palm for how) to make this activity even more fun!

GUIDED READING: NONFICTION

Here are lessons for two nonfiction books: *Footprints in the Snow* by Cynthia Benjamin (Cartwheel, 1994) is an easy book that works well for first grade. *Snow Is Falling* by Franklyn M. Branley (HarperTrophy, 2000) is a book second or third graders could easily read and learn from.

FOOTPRINTS IN THE SNOW
BEFORE READING

Say to students, "Snow falls in winter. Who is making footprints in the snow?" Then, let students make some predictions while you write what they say. Next, read the book to find out if students' predictions are correct.

DURING READING (ECHO READING)

Read the sentences, words, or phrases on each page aloud. Then, have students become your echo and read the same text after you.

AFTER READING

Were any of their predictions correct? Discuss what happened in this book: Who hops? Where did he go? Who runs? Who stomps? Where did she go? Who swims? Where does he go? Who races? Where does she go? Who flies? Where does he go? Who hurries? Where does she go? Who scampers? Where does he go? Who walks? Where does she go?

If there is time the same day or on the following day, have your students read this story again—by themselves.

SNOW

SNOW IS FALLING

BEFORE READING

Discuss any facts that students in your class know about snow.

DURING READING (INDEPENDENT OR PARTNER READING)

Let students read the book silently alone or whisper read it with partners. Give students some self-stick notes to mark and list three new things they learned when reading this book.

AFTER READING

Discuss what students learned while reading this book and make a list of the different facts they wrote on their sticky notes. For example:

- Snow covers plants and protects them from wind, ice, and the cold.

- Eskimos sometimes make houses called igloos out of snow.

- Melted snow gives us water.

- A blizzard makes life hard for animals and people.

- Snow is fun to play in.

WORKING WITH WORDS

MAKING WORDS

In these lessons, you dictate words, and students use small letter cards (or cut apart letter strips) to make these words. (The "secret" word is the last word made and uses all of the letters.) Next, lead students to sort the words for beginning sounds or spelling patterns. The final step is the transfer step. Have students use the sort patterns to decode and spell new words.

Making Words Letters: e, i, n, t, r, w ("secret" word: winter)

Make: in, win, tin, ten/net, tie, tire, wire, twin, went, wine, twine, write, winter

Sort: –in (in, win, tin, twin); –ine (wine, twine); –ire (tire, wire)

Transfer: skin, spin, spine, fire

Making Words Letters: a, o, m, n, n, s, w ("secret" word: snowman)

Make: so, no, am, an, man, Sam, saw, won/now/own, sown/snow, swam, woman, snowman

Sort: –an (an, man, woman, snowman); –am (am, Sam, swam); –own (own, sown)

Transfer: plan, jam, cram, grown

© CARSON-DELLOSA • INTEGRATING READING, WRITING, AND WORDS LESSONS • CD-104194

SNOW

Making Words Letters: a, o, b, l, l, n, s, w
("secret" word: snowball)

Make: as, was/saw, law, low, bow, bowl/blow, slow, snow, ball, balls, blows, blown, snowball

Sort: –aw (saw, law); –ow (low, bow, blow); plurals (balls, blows)

Transfer: claw, draw, grow, snowballs

ROUNDING UP THE RHYMES

Reread the book *The Biggest Snowball Fight* aloud to the class.

Stop after each set of rhymes (sometimes there are two sets on a page) and have students "round up the rhymes"—listen and tell you the rhyming words you have just read. Write the rhyming words on a board or on index cards that will be displayed in a pocket chart. You do not have to do all of the rhymes in this book—10 sets is about right, but it can be more or fewer.

tock	down	day	sound	clock
clock	town	McKay	around	shock
		play		

pants	around	wiggling	fun	McGee
dance	ground	jiggling	one	be
		giggling		

Next, call students' attention to the spelling patterns (how the rhymes are written). Get rid of any sets that do not have the same spelling pattern.

It will look like this:

tock	down	day	sound	clock
clock	town	McKay	around	shock
		play		

~~pants~~	around	wiggling	~~fun~~	~~McGee~~
~~dance~~	ground	jiggling	~~one~~	~~be~~
		giggling		

Finally, use these spelling patterns to read and write transfer words.

READING TRANSFER

Show students the following words, one at a time, written on separate index cards: **smock**, **clown**, and **found**. Show the words to students; don't say them. For each word, ask students, "What if I were reading and came to this word? Which words on the board would help me read it?" If students can't read the words on the index cards, hold each card under the words with the same pattern and read down (for example, **tock**, **clock**, **smock**).

WRITING TRANSFER

Write **block**, **stay**, and **hound** on the board or index cards. Ask students, "What if it was writing time and I wanted to write **block**? I rode my bike around the **block**. Which words on the board would help me write **block**? Yes, t-o-c-k and c-l-o-c-k." Have your students spell each word as you say it. If students can't spell the word, then put the blank index card under the words with the same pattern and stretch out the **b-l** as you write it. Then, finish the word with the pattern **–ock**.

GUESS THE COVERED WORD

Write the sentences below on an overhead transparency or piece of chart paper. (Write the name of a student on each line. This makes the activity even more fun!) Cover the bold word in each sentence with two, dark colored self-stick notes—one note to cover the "onset" (all of the consonants before the first vowel) and the other note to cover the "rime" (the rest of the word). Let students have four guesses and write these guesses on the transparency or chart paper. Then, uncover the onset. Let students guess again, if necessary. Students will use context clues, beginning letters (onsets), and word length to guess the covered words in these sentences.

IN WINTER . . .

1. _____ likes to **skate**.

2. _____ makes a **snowman**.

3. _____ wears a red **scarf**.

4. _____ likes to play **basketball**.

5. _____ gets to ride on a **snowplow**.

WRITING

Following is a mini-lesson that you could write on a piece of chart paper or transparency; it is about some things (facts) the children know or have learned about snow. The purpose of this lesson is to model for the entire class how to write an informational piece. As you write, share some things you know about snow and writing. Talk about how you begin each sentence with a capital letter and end each sentence with a period. Explain what you are going to say about snow and why you are writing it.

This is what the finished piece might look like in second or third grade.

Snow

In winter, it snows. When snow covers the ground it protects the plants from wind, ice, and the cold. The snow protects the animals that live underground in winter. People like snow. They like to go sledding and skiing and build snowmen. But, snow also means work. People have to shovel walks, plow streets, and dress warmly to go outside!

A first-grade piece would be simpler:

Snow

In winter, it snows. People work in the snow. They shovel walks and plow streets.

People play in the snow. They go sledding and skiing. Sometimes, they build a snowman.

QUICK WRITES OR OTHER IDEAS FOR WRITING MINI-LESSONS

Here are a few Quick Writes that can be posted in the room so that children will have writing activities to work on. These ideas also could be used for other mini-lessons while learning about snow.

- Some people like to build snowmen when it snows. Write the steps for building a snowman.

- Write about a time you were in a snowball fight.

- Describe your favorite snow activity.

FOOD ACTIVITY

HOT CHOCOLATE

INGREDIENTS

- Hot chocolate mix
- Warm water

- Marshmallows or marshmallow cream or whipped cream

- Graham crackers or cookies (optional)

DIRECTIONS

1. Follow the directions on the hot chocolate mix box, but use warm water to avoid burns.

2. Let students stir their own cups of hot chocolate. For an even more special treat, add marshmallows, marshmallow cream, or whipped cream. You could also provide graham crackers or snowman-shaped cookies.

Caution: Before completing any food activity, ask families' permission and inquire about students' food allergies and religious or other food preferences.

ART ACTIVITY

SNOWMAN COLLAGES

MATERIALS

- 18" x 24" bright blue construction paper
- Scissors
- Construction paper or paint in a variety of other colors
- White construction paper or white paint
- Glue sticks

DIRECTIONS

1. Give each student a piece of bright blue construction paper for the background.

2. Encourage students to use white construction paper (or white paint) to make snowmen.

3. Let students use the other supplies to decorate their snowmen by adding hats, faces, scarves, coats, etc.

4. Display the snowman collages proudly where the whole school can see and admire them.

CULMINATING ACTIVITY

SNOW DAY

- Let students watch a winter video or movie—perhaps the well-liked tale of *Frosty the Snowman* (Rankin and Bass, 1969).

- Serve students a winter snack of hot chocolate with cookies or graham crackers while they watch the video.

VACATION

What's the first word that pops into your head when you hear the words "summer vacation"? Traveling? Most vacations involve loading the car and hitting the road to visit family or friends. Although summer is a time when many people take vacations, Labor Day is the most celebrated vacation weekend in America. It is the "last blast" of summer fun, and, for many students, it is the last day of freedom before they go back to school.

Despite the number of people you might know who take their children on family vacations, there are plenty of children who never have the opportunity to go to beaches, mountains, amusement parks, or relatives' houses. Encourage students to relate vacationing to having fun with their families. For those children who don't pile into the car and head for the Grand Canyon or fly to Orlando to visit Disney World®, help them to see that a few hours at a video arcade or a day at the local public pool is, in essence, a mini-vacation.

SELF-SELECTED READING

Books for teachers to read aloud and then put in book baskets or on shelves for Self-Selected Reading:

FICTION

Cam Jansen and the Mystery of the Carnival Prize by David A. Adler (Puffin Books, 2004)
When Cam Jansen notices that people are just walking away with prizes from the dime toss, supposedly the most difficult game, she puts her sleuthing skills to the test.

Cam Jansen and the Mystery of the Circus Clown by David A. Adler (Puffin Books, 2004)
When Cam Jansen's aunt's wallet disappears, clues point to a clown, who also seems to have disappeared. Cam and her friend Eric solve the mystery.

Arthur's Family Vacation by Marc Brown (Little, Brown and Company, 1993)
Even though Arthur wants to go to camp with his friend, he and his family take a vacation instead. Arthur is miserable in the tiny hotel room watching the rain, but he eventually begins to plan family outings to a fudge factory, the movies, and even a jungle cruise. On the very last day of the trip, the sun finally shines, and the family enjoys a little time on the beach after all.

Clifford Takes a Trip by Norman Bridwell (Cartwheel, 1992)
Unhappy to be left at home when the family takes a vacation, Clifford sets out to find them so that he can enjoy his usual summer fun.

Emma's Vacation by David McPhail (Scholastic, Inc., 1994)
Different people have different ideas about what makes a good vacation. Emma's parents' idea of a good time is to take a car drive, a bus ride, boat trips, and train rides. All of these plans make everyone tired, so Emma helps her parents learn how to relax and have fun on vacation.

Fluffy's Spring Vacation by Kate McMullan (Rebound by Sagebrush, 2001)
Emma gets to take Fluffy the class guinea pig home for spring break. Feline residents Jack and Jill are very interested in Fluffy, but Skippy the dog comes to the rescue.

Martha Calling by Susan Meddaugh (Houghton Mifflin Company, 1996) Martha the talking dog calls a radio station and wins a four-day vacation at the Come-On-Inn! Martha gets around the "no dogs" policy (for a while) by dressing as a grandmother in a wheelchair.

The Night Before Summer Vacation by Natasha Wing (Grosset & Dunlap, 2002)
Inspired by the familiar Christmas poem, a little girl describes her family's frantic last minute preparations for summer vacation. Illustrator Julie Durrell captures the excitement and anticipation of the final moments before taking a summer trip.

My Family Vacation by Dayal Kaur Khalsa (Tundra Books, 2003)
May, her parents, and her older brother Richie drive off to Florida for a vacation. May squabbles with her brother Richie, looks for the perfect souvenirs, and enjoys motel swimming pools.

NONFICTION OR INFORMATIONAL BOOKS

Fair! by Ted Lewin (HarperCollins Publishers, 1997)
Lewin describes the food, amusements, and displays of a county fair. Beautiful watercolors show children receiving blue ribbons, prize-winning livestock, and the set up and breakdown of the fair.

AAA Beach Vacation Travel Journal with Stephen A. Leatherman (AAA Publishing, 2003)
AAA's Journal Guides™ are creative travel journals that let children get more involved with their vacations. Children can jot down notes, as well as attach photographs and postcards. This guide includes facts and trivia about 30 U. S. beaches, such as information on local birds and animals and kid-friendly activities.

VACATION

GUIDED READING

Just a Snowy Vacation by Gina and Mercer Mayer (Golden Books, 2004) is a good story for reading in first grade during the winter months or as an easier selection for second grade. These same activities could be done with Marc Brown's *Arthur's Family Vacation* (Little, Brown and Company, 1993) in a second-grade class or as an easier selection for third-grade students.

BEFORE READING

Tell students they are going to read a story about a family that takes a road trip to a ski resort in the mountains. Talk about text-to-self connections. Ask students, "Have you gone on a skiing vacation?" Display a map and let students tell about different places where they have been on skiing vacations or any other vacations. Discuss the different ways they traveled to their destinations (cars, airplanes, etc.). If skiing is not a common activity in your area, take a picture walk and talk about the winter pictures and what the family is doing in each one.

VOCABULARY

- vacation
- mountain
- bellhop
- critter
- breakfast
- rental booth
- bunny slope
- rescue team
- slopes
- bandage
- comfy
- ski lift

DURING READING: (PARTNER READING)

If you are a first-grade teacher, the first reading could be an Echo Reading—read a page and then have students become the echo, reading the same page after you. The second reading in first grade and the initial reading in second grade could be Partner Reading. Assign partners—top students with the average readers, average readers or

"good teachers" with the struggling readers. Have students read to find out the characters, setting, and what happened in the story. Tell them to discuss these with their partners when they finish reading.

AFTER READING

Discuss the story and fill in the Story Map together with students or toss the Beach Ball (page 28) and have students answer the questions.

The Story Map might look like this:

Title and Author: Just a Snowy Vacation by Gina and Mercer Mayer

Setting: Critter Mountain Ski Resort

Characters: Little Critter, his mother, father, and sister are the main characters in this book. There are other characters: Grandma, the baby, the bellhop, the doctor, the rescue team, etc.

Beginning: The family leaves the baby at Grandma's house and drives to the ski resort.

Middle: The family does many things at the resort. First, they rent skis. Then, Mom and Dad leave the children at the bunny slope and go off to ski. Dad hurts his ankle and the doctor has to bandage it. The little critters also ice skate while their parents watch.

End: The family packs up, the bellhop loads the car, and Mom drives them home.

WORKING WITH WORDS

MAKING WORDS

In these lessons, you dictate words, and students use small letter cards (or cut apart letter strips) to make these words. (The "secret" word is the last word made and uses all of the letters.) Next, lead students to sort the words for beginning sounds or spelling patterns. The final step is the transfer step. Have students use the sort patterns to decode and spell new words.

Making Words Letters: a, e, i, g, l, n, r, t, v ("secret" word: traveling)

Make: in, an, at, ate/eat, tin, ten/net, ran, van, let, get, gin, grin/ring, give, live, line, gave, rain, gain, grain, train, gravel, travel, traveling

Sort: –in (in, tin, gin, grin); –an (an, ran, van); –ain (gain, rain, grain, train)

Transfer: win, spin, plan, explain

Making Words Letters: e, e, i, c, l, n, s ("secret" word: license)

Make: is, in, sin, lie, ice, lens, else, lice, nice, line, lines, ices, seen, scene, niece, since, senile, silence/license

Sort: –in (in, sin); –ice (ice, nice, lice); plurals (lens, lines, ices); homonyms (seen, scene)

Transfer: spin, twice, nieces, scenes

Making Words Letters: a, o, c, d, p, r, s, t ("secret" word: postcard)

Make: ad, sad, tad, tap, car, par, tar, top, stop/post/pots, card, star, scar, trap, toad, soap, coast, roast, strap, scrap, traps, drops, postcard

Sort: –ad (ad, sad, tad); –ar (par, tar, car, star, scar); –op (stop, top); –ap (tap, trap, strap, scrap); –oast (coast, roast)

Transfer: dad, far, slop, slap, toast

GUESS THE COVERED WORD

Write the following sentences on an overhead transparency or piece of chart paper. Cover the bold word in each sentence with two, dark colored self-stick notes—one note to cover the "onset" (all of the consonants before the first vowel) and the other note to cover the "rime" (the rest of the word). Let students have four guesses and write these guesses on the transparency or chart paper. Then, uncover the onset. Let students guess again, if necessary. Students will use context clues, beginning letters (onsets), and word length to guess the covered words in these sentences.

VACATION

VACATION TRIP

1. We are going on a road trip to vacation at the **lake**.

2. I am excited because we are going to stay in a **hotel**.

3. We will visit our **friends**.

4. I made sure that I packed my **games**.

5. We have **books** to occupy our time while traveling.

WRITING

Going on vacation usually involves travel. Get your students excited to write about their travels with this activity.

Using a wall map of the country, state, or province that you live in, call on students who are interested in showing where they have been on vacations. If a student doesn't know where to find a place on the map, you may be able to find it for her. Mark each location with a small self-stick note so that everyone can see the many places students in the class have been for vacations. Then, have each student write about a vacation spot she has been to. However, some students have never been on a vacation—last summer or any summer! In this case, you may want to do an alternate assignment.

Call each student to the front of the room, one at a time, to be blindfolded. Once the student is blindfolded, spin him around a few times while the class chants, "Hurry, hurry, we're on our way. Our vacation starts today! Where it's at we don't know, but in just a second, we will go!" Guide the student to the map and have him point to a location. Take off the blindfold and tell the student where he is headed on his vacation.

Once all of the students have chosen a place to go, they will need to get some background information on their vacation destinations so that they can plan their adventures. If you have a teacher's assistant or parent volunteer in the classroom, they can work one-on-one with each student to help her get information from the Internet.

If you have limited technology resources, have one student choose a place that the entire class will focus on. This allows you to look up the information and provide all of the students with the same basic information from which to write their vacation stories.

Students can write their stories and then glue them onto luggage-shaped pieces of construction paper. Or, they can compile the stories into a class vacation book. After gathering all of the final copies, place them in a cover that resembles a piece of luggage. Place the book with other Self-Selected Reading books and let students enjoy the stories written by their peers.

VACATION

QUICK WRITES OR OTHER IDEAS FOR WRITING MINI-LESSONS

Here are a few Quick Writes that can be posted in the room so that children will have writing activities to work on. These ideas also could be used for other mini-lessons while learning about vacations.

- Write about a vacation that you took with your family.

- Make a travel poster about a vacation destination of your choice.

- Write about what you can do to pass the time while traveling in a car.

FOOD ACTIVITY

LICENSE PLATES

INGREDIENTS

- ½ cup butter
- ½ cup shortening
- 1½ cup granulated sugar
- 2 eggs
- 1 tsp vanilla
- 4 tsp baking powder
- 1 tsp salt
- 3¾ cup flour
- 3 tbsp milk
- Tube frosting

DIRECTIONS

1. Cream butter and shortening thoroughly.

2. Add sugar and beat well.

3. Add eggs and vanilla. Blend.

4. Add remaining dry ingredients alternately with milk.

5. Mix and chill dough; then, roll out (not too thin).

6. Cut the dough into rectangles.

7. Bake at 400° F for 6–8 minutes.

8. After the cookies cool, have students decorate them with tube frosting to make personalized license plates (for example, CUTIE, GR8, 2COOL, or 4REAL).

Caution: Before completing any food activity, ask families' permission and inquire about students' food allergies and religious or other food preferences.

VACATION

ART ACTIVITY

MAKING POSTCARDS

Have students look through travel magazines and cut out scenes from vacation destinations. Let them glue their pictures onto index cards to make postcards. Have students write to friends about their "pretend" vacation spots.

CULMINATING ACTIVITY

Set up mini-vacation centers in your classroom. Divide students into groups of three to six (depending on the total number of students) and give each group a disposable camera to share. Let students visit the centers, complete the activities, and take pictures while they are in the centers. In each center, provide fiction and nonfiction books related to the vacation spot for students to enjoy. This could be a half-day activity or students could visit a different center every day for a week. Develop the pictures and let students make a class vacation scrapbook.

- Beach: Children can do a shell sort. Provide sand toys, such as buckets and shovels, and clean sand in a plastic tub for students to stand in or play with. Let them toss around a beach ball.

- Mountains: Children can do leaf rubbings and compare bark and moss. Make a trail for them to follow around the back of the classroom.

- Lake: Have a tub of water set up with different objects. Let students explore sinking and floating. Use a rug for a pretend lake and let students go fishing. Attach string to yardsticks for "poles" and add magnet "hooks." Cut out fish shapes and attach a paper clip to each. You could write spelling words, vocabulary words, or even math facts on the fish.

- Amusement Park: Let the children build and explore with interlocking plastic blocks. They can set up and knock down dominoes, too.

- Souvenir Shop: Have various objects marked with price tags. Let children use play money to count and pay for the objects. The shop could also be a rest stop with snacks. Provide bags of chips and juice boxes.

ZOO

Do you live in or near a big city? Then, you might live near a zoo. Many states have zoos, but not all students live close enough to visit them. Going to the zoo can be a cherished family tradition if there is one within driving distance. Children can experience prairie dogs going in and out of their holes, polar bears swimming in frigid water, or bats flying through darkened caves. Zoos help make children aware of the connections between humans and Earth's animals, plants, and other natural resources. It is important that students have an understanding and appreciation of the wonderful diversity of nature that surrounds them.

Despite the numerous zoos around the world, many children have never experienced the thrills of seeing animals living in habitats similar to their native ones. Children can sometimes see and touch animals at petting zoos, but the variety of animals is limited. A full-sized zoo brings a wonderful menagerie from all over the world to one place. Children can learn so much by visiting a zoo. If your students have not or cannot visit a zoo, read about animals or show videos of animals in zoos or their natural habitats. A visit to any zoo is thrilling no matter what!

SELF-SELECTED READING

Books for teachers to read aloud and then put in book baskets or on shelves for Self-Selected Reading:

FICTION

Good Night, Gorilla by Peggy Rathmann (Putman Juvenile, 1996)
As a zookeeper walks through the zoo to say good night to all of the animals, a gorilla with a set of stolen keys follows behind him and frees the animals. The animals then follow the zookeeper all the way home and right into bed!

Birthday Zoo by Deborah Lee Rose (Albert Whitman and Company, 2002)
Twenty-three different animals conspire to make a great birthday party for a little boy. Each animal's efforts rhyme with its name.

Corduroy at the Zoo by Don Freeman (Viking Juvenile, 2001)
As Corduroy and his friends take a trip to the zoo, young readers can lift the flaps and find surprises throughout the book. Animals hide in different locations and provide extra entertainment.

If I Ran the Zoo by Dr. Seuss (Random House Books for Young Readers, 1977)
Dr. Seuss works his magic when a little boy imagines replacing all of the zoo animals with new, more fanciful creatures.

Curious George Visits the Zoo by Margret Rey (Houghton Mifflin Company, 1985)
Curious George starts off his zoo visit on the wrong foot by stealing some bananas but saves the day by rescuing a little boy's escaping balloon.

We're Going to the Zoo by Lorraine Gallacher (Simon Spotlight/Nickelodeon, 2001)
Little Bill, a Bill Cosby creation, joins his friends on a trip to the zoo. Colorful illustrations and stickers add to the enjoyment of this book.

Young Cam Jansen and the Zoo Note Mystery by David A. Adler (Puffin Books, 2004)
As Cam and Eric prepare to go on a class field trip to the local zoo, Eric realizes that his permission slip is missing. If he can't find it, he will have to sit in the principal's office all day while the other children go to the zoo! Cam and Eric put their heads together to ensure that Eric can go on the field trip.

Young Cam Jansen and the Mystery at the Monkey House by David A. Adler (Viking, 1985)
Cam Jansen and her sidekick Eric think someone is stealing monkeys from the Jackson Park Zoo. Once again, Cam is able to use her photographic memory to find the thief and save the missing monkeys.

NONFICTION OR INFORMATIONAL BOOKS

Zookeepers Care for Animals by Amy Moses (Child's World, 1996)
This book follows zookeepers to show how they care for different types of animals. Zoo animals are depicted in colorful photographs.

ZOO

GUIDED READING

Zoo-Looking by Mem Fox (Mondo Publishing, 1996) is a wonderful Guided Reading book and works well for a variety of reading levels.

BEFORE READING

Teach students the following chant/song:

> Daddy's taking us to the zoo tomorrow, zoo tomorrow, zoo tomorrow.
>
> Daddy's taking us to the zoo tomorrow, and we can stay all day.
>
> We're going to the zoo, zoo, zoo.
>
> How about you, you, you?
>
> You can come too, too, too.
>
> We're going to the zoo, zoo, zoo.

Brainstorm with students a list of animals that Flora might see when she visits the zoo. Then, take a picture walk to see which animals she does see.

Write the names of the animals from the book on index cards. Punch a hole in the top corners of each index card. Create a word card necklace by tying a loop of yarn through the two holes.

Call students to the front of the classroom and hang the word card necklaces around their necks. Start out with three necklaces. Have the rest of the class put the animals in the same order in which Flora saw them at the zoo. Add more animals until students can arrange all of the necklace wearers in the correct order.

DURING READING

This is an easy text with rhyming words that can be read by the whole class as a Choral Reading. Read the text all together the first time and then assign certain pages to groups of children to read together.

AFTER READING

Have students act out the book. Add word card necklaces for Flora and Dad. Assign all of the parts and hang the necklaces around the necks of the "actors." There are 16 action parts. Assign the part of Narrator to the rest of the class. They will read the parts of the book that aren't in quotation marks.

ZOO

WORKING WITH WORDS

MAKING WORDS

In these lessons, you dictate words, and students use small letter cards (or cut apart letter strips) to make these words. (The "secret" word is the last word made and uses all of the letters.) Next, lead students to sort the words for beginning sounds or spelling patterns. The final step is the transfer step. Have students use the sort patterns to decode and spell new words.

Making Words Letters: a, e, e, h, l, n, p, s, t ("secret" word: elephants)

Make: an, at, as, pan, tan, ate/eat, sat, hat, pat, see, set, pet, ten/net, pea, sea, eel, sale, pale, east/seat, hate/heat, peel, steel, steal, tease, easel, please, elephants

Sort: –at (at, sat, pat, hat); –et (set, pet, net); –an (an, pan, tan); –eel (eel, peel, steel); –eat (eat, heat, seat); homonyms (see, sea; steal, steel)

Transfer: brat, met, plan, reel, meat

Making Words Letters: a, e, o, d, l, p, r, s ("secret" word: leopards)

Make: old, led, lad, pad, sad, rod, sod, sold, sop, slop, rope, soap, read/dear, road, rode, load, leap, deal, real, seal/sale, drop, drops, drape, drapes, leopards

Sort: –ad (sad, pad, lad); –od (sod, rod); –old (old, sold); –eal (seal, real, deal); –op (sop, slop, drop)

Transfer: fad, cod, bold, veal, cop

Making Words Letters: e, o, y, k, m, n, s ("secret" word: monkeys)

Make: on/no, so, my, sky, son, men, yes, Ken, key, soy, keys, yoke, some, smoke, monkey, monkeys

Sort: –y (my, sky); –en (men, Ken); –oke (yoke, smoke)

Transfer: try, den, broke

ZOO

GUESS THE COVERED WORD

Write the sentences below on an overhead transparency or piece of chart paper. Cover the bold word in each sentence with two, dark colored self-stick notes—one note to cover the "onset" (all of the consonants before the first vowel) and the other note to cover the rime (the rest of the word). Let students have four guesses and write these guesses on the transparency or chart paper. Then, uncover the onset. Let students guess again, if necessary. Students will use context clues, beginning letters (onsets), and word length to guess the covered words in these sentences.

AT THE ZOO

1. Don't **feed** the animals.

2. My favorite exhibit is the **monkeys**.

3. There are many **species** of birds in the aviary.

4. The **seals** play and splash in the water.

5. The new habitats have **trees** instead of just concrete and cages.

WRITING

In the same way you teach students to add numbers when regrouping by using manipulatives and teaching the steps, you must also teach students to write by modeling the steps. All too often, teachers give students a topic and send them off to write. However, in order to help students become great writers, you must make sure they understand that stories have elements, such as characters, setting, plot, etc. This writing lesson focuses on teaching those concepts using a step-by-step approach.

First, have students cut out pictures from magazines that show animals you might find in a zoo (monkeys, birds, large cats, elephants, etc.). Next, have students cut out pictures of places people can go (castles, islands, amusement parks, planets, jungles, etc.). Finally, have them look for pictures of people dealing with real or imaginary problems or challenges (doing homework, cooking dinner, playing soccer, having an argument, flying a plane, etc.). These actions can be difficult for children to see in pictures, so you might have them illustrate pictures instead and then write the plot (what is going on in the picture) at the bottom.

For the next step, collect all of the pictures and place them in separate boxes labeled **Character**, **Setting**, and **Plot**. (Note: If your class is not ready for the word **plot**, you can use the words **Problem and Solution** instead.)

Explain that the author gets to choose who the characters are in the story. This allows the author to choose who becomes the hero and who becomes the villain. Ask one student to select two pictures from the **Character** box and attach them to the board or place them in a pocket chart. Then, ask the student to name the two characters. For example, the student might select a giraffe (George) and a hippo (Tina).

Explain that stories can magically whisk the reader away to new or faraway places. These places are called settings. When an author writes a story, she takes herself and her readers to any place or setting she wants. An author can help her readers feel like they have really traveled to a place by describing what it looks like, how it smells, how it feels, how it sounds, or even how it tastes. Then, ask a student to select a picture from the **Setting** box. For example, a student might select a picture of the beach. Together, students determine the setting is the Bahamas.

Next, ask students, "Are characters and setting all that you need for a story?" After listening to their responses, tell them that most stories start with a problem that the main character (hero) must solve. The problem is usually caused by another character (villain). Explain that a story's plot can be any kind of problem—an ordinary everyday problem or an extraordinary problem. The main part of the story will be the hero trying to solve the problem. This is known as the plot. The hero usually won't solve the problem on the first couple of tries but keeps trying until the problem is solved and the villain is defeated. Explain that the initial problem, the hero's attempts to try to solve the problem, and the ultimate resolution of the problem all comprise the story's plot. Have another student select a picture from the **Plot** box. For example, the student might select a picture of a car with its hood raised and say that the car has broken down.

Finally, display the three pictures in a row and model writing a story using the three elements that students have provided. You may choose to have students help get the ideas together or simply stick to modeling

and thinking out loud.

George and Tina

Being an animal in the zoo is tough because people stare at you all day long. George the giraffe and Tina the hippo decided they needed a vacation.

On Friday, George rented a car and asked Tina to go on a trip with him. Tina wanted to go to the Bahamas. So, George loaded all of their stuff into the car. Tina was supposed to check the oil.

They started the car's engine and drove down the dusty highway. After 20 miles, the engine started to smoke. Finally, the engine stopped, and they pulled over. The car was out of oil, and George was mad.

After they fixed the engine, they arrived in the Bahamas. They had a great vacation and were ready to go back to the zoo again.

This lesson can be followed on another day by allowing students to do the same activity on their own. You may find that you need to draw a plot picture and tell them what problem it represents. This may make it easier to monitor the flow of the stories and keep children focused on the main topic (the zoo). Allow students to draw their own character and setting pictures. As students become more comfortable with this fun way of making a story come alive, you can allow them more autonomy.

ZOO

QUICK WRITES OR OTHER IDEAS FOR WRITING MINI-LESSONS

Here are a few Quick Writes that can be posted in the room so that children will have writing activities to work on. These ideas also could be used for other mini-lessons while learning about zoos.

- Describe your favorite zoo animal.

- Pretend you woke up fenced in at the zoo. Describe your habitat.

- Design and draw a map of a zoo. What animals would you have? Where would you place them?

FOOD ACTIVITY

ANIMAL CRACKER CAROUSELS

INGREDIENTS

- Apples (one per student)
- Peanut butter
- Drinking straws
- Animal crackers

DIRECTIONS

1. Cut the apples in half.

2. Have students spread peanut butter on both sides of their apples.

3. Help students cut each drinking straw into three even pieces.

4. Have each student place one apple half on the table (peanut butter up). Then, have each student push four straw pieces through the peanut butter into his apple. The straws should form the corners of a square. Finally, have each student carefully place the other apple half on top of the four straw pieces (peanut butter down). This will create a "carousel."

5. Have each student select four animal crackers and place them in the peanut butter on the bottom half of the apple between the straws to complete their carousels.

6. Let students enjoy their Animal Cracker Carousels with juice, milk, or water.

Caution: Before completing any food activity, ask families' permission and inquire about students' food allergies and religious or other food preferences.

ART ACTIVITY

ILLUSTRATION

Have students illustrate their favorite zoo animals in their natural habitats on letter-sized paper. Then, have them cut thin strips of black construction paper and glue the strips on top of the picture to create bars for their animal enclosures.

CULMINATING ACTIVITY

ZOO DAY

- Have students make zoo animal masks using paper plates, yarn, and a variety of art supplies. Celebrate with an animal parade and invite other classes to watch.

- Let students dance to the song "Do the Monkey" by The Wiggles (*Yummy, Yummy*, Koch Records, 2003). Let students demonstrate how each animal would act and/or sound.

- Have students look at, sort, and sample animal crackers.

REFERENCES

PROFESSIONAL REFERENCES

• A •

- Anderson, R. C., and P. D. Pearson. 1984. A schema-theoretical view: Basic process in reading comprehension. *Handbook of Reading Research*. Edited by P. D. Pearson et al. (255–291). Hillsdale, NJ: Laurence Erlbaum Associates.

• B •

- Beyer, B. K. 1985. Teaching critical thinking: A direct approach. *Social Education* 49: 297–303.
- Bruner, J. S. 1986. *Actual Minds, Possible Worlds*. Cambridge: Cambridge University Press.

• C •

- Calkins, L. M. 1994. *The Art of Teaching Writing*. Portsmouth, NH: Heinemann Publishing.
- Costa, A. L., ed. 1985. Teacher behaviors that enable student thinking. *Developing Minds: A Resource Book for Teaching Thinking* (125–137). Alexandria, VA: Association for Supervision and Curriculum Development.
- Cunningham, P. M., and D. P. Hall. 2003, 1997. *Month-by-Month Phonics for First Grade*. Greensboro, NC: Carson-Dellosa Publishing.
- Cunningham, P. M. and D. P. Hall. 2003, 1998. *Month-by-Month Phonics for Third Grade*. Greensboro, NC: Carson-Dellosa Publishing.
- Cunningham, P. M., D. P. Hall, and J. W. Cunningham. 2002. *Guided Reading the Four-Blocks® Way*. Greensboro, NC: Carson-Dellosa Publishing.
- Cunningham, P. M., D. P. Hall, and J. W. Cunningham. 2005. *Writing the Four-Blocks® Way*. Greensboro, NC: Carson-Dellosa Publishing.
- Cunningham, P. M., D. P. Hall, and L. B. Gambrell. 2002. *Self-Selected Reading the Four-Blocks® Way*. Greensboro, NC: Carson-Dellosa Publishing.

• G •

- Goodman, K. S. 1987. *Whole Language*. Portsmouth, NH: Heinemann Publishing.

• H •

- Hall, D. P., and P. M. Cunningham. 2003, 1998. *Month-by-Month Phonics for Second Grade*. Greensboro, NC: Carson-Dellosa Publishing.

REFERENCES

- Harris, T. L., and R. E. Hodges, eds. 1995. *The Literacy Dictionary*. Newark, DE: International Reading Association.

• —————— • **R** • ——————•

- Rumelhart, D. E. 1980. Schema: The building blocks of cognition. *Theoretical Issues in Reading Comprehension*. Edited by R. J. Spiro et al. (33–58). Hillsdale, NJ: Lawrence Erlbaum Associates.

• —————— • **T** • ——————•

- Tierney R. J., and P. D. Pearson. 1994. A framework for improving classroom practice. *Theoretical Models and Processes of Reading*. 4th ed. Edited by R. B. Ruddell et al. (496–513). Newark, DE: International Reading Association.

• —————— • **V** • ——————•

- Vygotsky, L. S. 1978. *Mind in Society: The Development of Higher Psychological Processes*. Cambridge, MA: Harvard University Press.

• —————— • **W** • ——————•

- Wells, G. 1986. *The Meaning Makers: Children Learning Language and Using Language to Learn*. Portsmouth, NH: Heinemann Publishing.

CHILDREN'S WORKS CITED

• —————— • **A** • ——————•

- *AAA Beach Vacation Travel Journal* with Stephen P. Leatherman (AAA Publishing, 2003).
- *ABC NYC: A Book of Seeing New York City* by Joanne Dugan (Harry N. Abrams, Inc., 2005).
- *The Adventures of Taxi Dog* by Debra and Sal Barracca (Dial, 1990).
- *Airplanes* by Lola Schaefer (Bridgestone Books, 1999).
- *Airport* by Byron Barton (HarperTrophy, 1987).
- *Alexander, Who's Not (Do You Hear Me? I Mean It!) Going to Move* by Judith Viorst (Aladdin, 1998).
- *All You Need for the Beach* by Alice Schertle (Silver Whistle, 2004).
- *Alphabet City* by Stephen T. Johnson (Puffin Books, 1999).
- *Amanda Pig and Her Best Friend Lollipop* by Jean Van Leeuwen (Puffin Books, 2000).
- *Amazing Rain* by Sam Brown (Soft Skull Press, 2004).
- *Amelia Bedelia Goes Camping* by Peggy Parish (HarperTrophy, 2003).
- *Amelia and Eleanor Go for a Ride* by Pam Muñoz Ryan (Scholastic Press, 1999).
- *Amelia's Road* by Linda Jacobs Altman (Lee & Low Books, 1995).
- *Anansi Goes Fishing* retold by Eric Kimmel (Holiday House, 1993).

- *Angela's Airplane* by Robert Munsch (Annick Press, 1988).
- *Apples* by Gail Gibbons (Holiday House, 2000).
- *Apples* by Ken Robbins (Atheneum, 2002).
- *Apples and Pumpkins* by Anne Rockwell (Aladdin, 1994).
- *Apples, Apples, Apples* by Nancy Elizabeth Wallace (Marshal Cavendish Corporation, 2004).
- *The Apple Pie Tree* by Zoe Hall (Blue Sky Press, 1996).
- *Arthur and the School Pet* by Marc Brown (Random House Books for Young Readers, 2003).
- *Arthur Goes to Camp* by Marc Brown (Little, Brown and Company, 1984).
- *Arthur's Family Vacation* by Marc Brown (Little, Brown and Company, 1993).
- *Arthur's First Sleepover* by Marc Brown (Little, Brown and Company, 1996).
- *Arthur's Pet Business* by Marc Brown (Little, Brown and Company, 1993).

• ———————— • **B** • ————————— •

- *Bailey Goes Camping* by Kevin Henkes (HarperTrophy, 1997).
- *Bathtime for Biscuit* by Alyssa Satin Capucilli (HarperTrophy, 1999).
- *Bear on a Bike* by Stella Blackstone (Barefoot Books, 2001).
- *The Bear's Picnic* by Stan and Jan Berenstain (Random House Books for Young Readers, 1966).
- *The Berenstain Bears Go to Camp* by Stan and Jan Berenstain (Random House Books for Young Readers, 1982).
- *The Berenstain Bears' Moving Day* by Stan and Jan Berenstain (Random House Books for Young Readers, 1981).
- *The Best Picnic Ever* by Clare Jarrett (Candlewick Press, 2004).
- *The Bicycle Man* by Allen Say (Houghton Mifflin Company, 1989).
- *Big Bird's Big Bike* by Anna Ross (Random House Books for Young Readers, 1993).
- *The Big Dig: Reshaping an American City* by Peter Vanderwarker (Little, Brown and Company, 2001).
- *The Big Fish: An Alaskan Fairy Tale* by Marie Wakeland (Misty Mountain, 1993).
- *The Biggest Snowball Fight!* by Angela Shelf Medearis (Scholastic Inc., 2003).
- *The Bike Lesson* by Stan and Jan Berenstain (Random House Books for Young Readers, 1964).
- *Birthday Zoo* by Deborah Lee Rose (Albert Whitman and Company, 2002).
- *Bringing the Rain to Kapiti Plain* by Verne Aardema (Puffin Books, 1992).
- *Busy, Busy Town* by Richard Scarry (Golden Books, 2000).

REFERENCES

• C •

- *Cam Jansen and the Mystery at the Monkey House* by David A. Adler (Puffin Books, 2004).
- *Cam Jansen and the Mystery of the Babe Ruth Baseball* by David A. Adler (Puffin Books, 2004).
- *Cam Jansen and the Mystery of the Carnival Prize* by David A. Adler (Puffin Books, 2004).
- *Cam Jansen and the Mystery of the Circus Clown* by David A. Adler (Puffin Books, 2004).
- *Cam Jansen and the Mystery of the Dinosaur Bones* by David A. Adler (Puffin Books, 2004).
- *Camping* by Tim Seeberg (Child's World, 2004).
- *Camping Out* by Mercer Mayer (School Specialty Publishing, 2001).
- *The Case of the Best Pet Ever* by James Preller (Scholastic Paperbacks, 2003).
- *The Case of the Spooky Sleepover* by James Preller (Scholastic Paperbacks, 2001).
- *The Chalk Box Kid* by Clyde Robert Bulla (Random House Books for Young Readers, 1987).
- *Clifford Takes a Trip* by Norman Bridwell (Cartwheel, 1992).
- *Clifford's Sports Day* by Norman Bridwell (Cartwheel, 1996).
- *Come On, Rain* by Karen Hesse (Scholastic Press, 1999).
- *Corduroy at the Zoo* by Don Freeman (Viking Juvenile, 2001).
- *Corduroy's Garden* by Alison Inches (Puffin Books, 2004).
- *Creative Sleepovers for Kids! Fun Activities, Themes, and Ideas for Overnight Parties for Boys or Girls* by Julie Kauffman (Prima Lifestyles, 2001).
- *Curious George and the Dinosaur* (Houghton Mifflin Company, 1989).
- *Curious George Goes to the Beach* (Houghton Mifflin Company, 1999).
- *Curious George Takes a Job* by H. A. Rey (Houghton Mifflin Company, 1974).
- *Curious George Visits the Zoo* by Margret Ray (Houghton Mifflin Company, 1985).

• D •

- *A Day in the Life of a Dentist* by Heather Adamson (Capstone Press, 2003).
- *Desert Rain* by Pat Malone (National Geographic Society, 2001).
- *Doctor De Soto* by William Steig (Farrar, Straus and Giroux, 1990).
- *Down Comes the Rain* by Franklyn M. Branley (HarperTrophy, 1997).
- *Dr. Jekyll, Orthodontist* by Dan Greenburg (Grosset & Dunlap, 1997).
- *Duck on a Bike* by David Shannon (Blue Sky Press, 2002).

• E •

- *Edward's Overwhelming Overnight* by Rosemary Wells (Dial Books for Young Readers, 1995).

REFERENCES

- *Eloise* by Kay Thompson (Simon & Schuster Children's Publishing, 1969).
- *Emma's Vacation* by David McPhail (Scholastic, Inc., 1994).
- *The Everything Kids Baseball Book: Star Players, Great Teams, Baseball Legends, and Tips on Playing Like a Pro* by Richard Mintzer (Adams Media Corporation, 2004).

• ———————————— • **F** • ———————————— •

- *Fireworks, Picnics, and Flags: The Story of the Fourth of July Symbols* by James Cross (Clarion Books, 2001).
- *The First Snowfall* by Anne and Harlow Rockwell (Aladdin, 1992).
- *Fish* by Steve Parker (DK Children, 2000).
- *Fish Story* by Katherine Andres (Simon & Schuster, 1993).
- *Fish Tales* by Nat Sagaloff and Paul Erickson (Sterling Publishing Company, Inc., 1990).
- *Fishing Day* by Andrea Davis Pinkney (Jump at the Sun, 2003).
- *Fluffy's Spring Vacation* by Kate McMullan (Rebound by Sagebrush, 2001).
- *Footprints in the Snow* by Cynthia Benjamin (Cartwheel, 1994).
- *Franklin Rides a Bike* by Paulette Bourgeois (Scholastic Paperbacks, 1997).
- *Franklin Wants a Pet* by Paulette Bourgeois (Scholastic Paperbacks, 1995).
- *From Seed to Plant* by Gail Gibbons (Holiday House, 1993).
- *Fruit* by Gallimard Jeanesse (Scholastic, Inc., 1991).

• ———————————— • **G** • ———————————— •

- *Gila Monsters Meet You at the Airport* by Marjorie Weinman Sharmat (Aladdin, 1990).
- *Glad Monster, Sad Monster: A Book About Feelings* by Ed Emberly and Anne Miranda (Little, Brown and Company, 1997).
- *A Good Day's Fishing* by James Prosek (Simon & Schuster Children's Publishing, 2004).
- *Good Night, Gorilla* by Peggy Rathmann (Putman Juvenile, 1996).
- *A Good Place to Live* by Marvin Buckley (National Geographic Society, 2001).
- *Good-Bye, 382 Shin Dang Dong* by Frances Park and Ginger Park (National Geographic Children's Books, 2002).
- *Growing Vegetable Soup* by Lois Elhert (Voyager Books, 1990).
- *Gus and Grandpa and the Two-Wheeled Bike* by Claudia Mills (Farrar, Strauss and Giroux, 2001).

• ———————————— • **H** • ———————————— •

- *Hachiko Waits* by Lesléa Newman (Henry Holt and Company, 2004).
- *Harry and the Dinosaurs at the Museum* by Ian Whybrow (Random House Books for Young Readers, 2005).

- *Henry and Mudge and Annie's Good Move* by Cynthia Rylant (Aladdin, 2000).
- *Henry and Mudge and the Starry Night* by Cynthia Rylant (Aladdin, 2000).
- *Here Comes the Snow* by Angela Shelf Medearis (Cartwheel, 1996).
- *Home* by Jeannie Baker (Greenwillow Books, 2004).
- *Hooray for Diffendoofer Day!* by Dr. Seuss, Jack Prelutsky, and Lane Smith (Knopf Books for Young Readers, 1998).
- *How Do Apples Grow?* by Betsy Maestro (HarperTrophy, 1993).
- *How Groundhog's Garden Grew* by Lynne Cherry (Blue Sky Press, 2003).
- *How Will We Get to the Beach?* by Brigitte Luciani (North-South Books, 2000).

• —————————— • I • —————————— •

- *I Can Go Camping* by Edana Eckart (Children's Press, 2003).
- *I Can Ride a Bike* by Edana Eckart (Children's Press, 2002).
- *I Love Guinea Pigs* by Dick King-Smith (Candlewick Press, 2001).
- *If I Ran the Zoo* by Dr. Suess (Random House Books for Young Readers, 1977).
- *I'm Not Moving, Mama!* by Nancy White Carlstrom (Aladdin, 1999).
- *Ira Says Goodbye* by Bernard Waber (Houghton Mifflin Company, 1988).
- *Iris and Walter: The Sleepover* by Elissa Haden Guest (Gulliver Books Paperbacks, 2003).

• —————————— • J • —————————— •

- *Johnny Appleseed* retold by Steven Kellogg (HarperCollins, 1988).
- *Julian's Glorious Summer* by Ann Cameron (Rebound by Sagebrush, 1999).
- *Junie B. Jones Smells Something Fishy* by Barbara Park (Random House Books for Young Readers, 1998).
- *Just a Snowy Vacation* by Gina and Mercer Mayer (Golden Books, 2004).
- *Just Fishing with Grandma* by Gina Mayer (Golden Books, 2003).
- *Just Going to the Dentist* by Mercer Mayer (Golden Books, 2001).
- *Just Me and My Puppy* by Mercer Mayer (Golden Books, 1998).

• —————————— • K • —————————— •

- *Katie and the Mona Lisa* by James Mayhew (Orchard Books, 1999).
- *Kids' Incredible Fishing Stories* by Shaun Morey (Workman Publishing Company, 1996).
- *Kumak's Fish: A Tall Tale from the Far North* by Michael Bania (Alaska Northwest Books, 2004).

• —————————— • L • —————————— •

- *Let's Go Froggy!* by Jonathan London (Puffin, 1996).

REFERENCES

- *Let's Go on a Picnic* by Cate Foley (Children's Press, 2001).
- *Let's Have a Slumber Party* (Barnes & Noble Books, 2002).
- *Lisa's Airplane Trip* by Anne Gutman (Knopf Books for Young Readers, 2001).
- *Listen to the Rain* by Bill Martin and John Archambault (Henry Holt and Company, 1988).
- *Little Rabbit's Loose Tooth* by Lucy Bate (Dragonfly Books, 1988).
- *Loading the Airplane* by Leslie Pether (National Geographic, 2001).

• M •

- *Martha Calling* by Susan Meddaugh (Houghton Mifflin Company, 1996).
- *Max* by Rachel Isadora (Aladdin Paperbacks, 1984).
- *Messy Bessey and the Birthday Overnight* by Patricia and Fredrick McKissack (Children's Press, 1999).
- *Messy Bessey's Garden!* by Patricia and Fredrick McKissack (Children's Press, 2002).
- *Mike and the Bike* by Michael Ward (Cookie Jar Publishing, 2005).
- *A Million Fish . . . More or Less* by Patricia McKissack (Dragonfly Books, 1996).
- *Miss Malarkey's Field Trip* by Judy Finchler and Kevin O'Malley (Walker Books for Young Readers, 2004).
- *Molly and the Slow Teeth* by Pat Ross (Houghton Mifflin Company, 1992).
- *Monk Camps Out* by Emily Arnold McCully (Arthur A. Levine Books, 2000).
- *Moving* by Janine Amos (Gareth Stevens Publishing, 2001).
- *The Moving Book: A Kids' Survival Guide* by Gabriel Davis (First Books, 2003).
- *Muncha! Muncha! Muncha!* by Candace Fleming (Atheneum/Anne Schwartz Books, 2002).
- *My Cat: How to Have a Happy, Healthy Pet* by Lynn Cole (Northwood Press, 2001).
- *My Family Vacation* by Dayal Kaur Khalsa (Tundra Books, 2003).
- *My Town at Work* by Gare Thompson (National Geographic Society, 2002).
- *My Visit to the Aquarium* by Aliki (HarperTrophy, 1996).
- *The Mystery of the Stolen Bike* by Marc Brown (Little, Brown and Company, 1998).

• N •

- *The Night Before Summer Vacation* by Natasha Wing (Grosset & Dunlap, 2002).
- *No, David!* by David Shannon (Blue Sky Press, 1998).
- *Norman the Doorman* by Don Freeman (Puffin Books, 2003).
- *Not Just Tutus* by Rachel Isadora (Putnam Juvenile, 2003).

• O •

- *The Ocean Alphabet Book* by Jerry Pallotta (Charlesbridge Publishing, 1986).

- *On My Beach There Are Many Pebbles* by Leo Lionni (HarperTrophy, 1995).
- *On the Way to the Beach* by Henry Cole (Greenwillow Books, 2003).
- *Open Wide!* by Tom Barber (Chrysalis Books Group, 2005).
- *Our Town* by Faridah Yusof (National Geographic Society, 2001).
- *Out and About at the Science Center* by Kitty Shea (Picture Window Books, 2004).
- *Out of the Ocean* by Debra Frasier (Voyager Books, 2002).

• —————————— • **P** • —————————— •

- *P. J. Funnybunny Camps Out* by Marilyn Sadler (Random House Books for Young Readers, 1994).
- *Park Rangers* by Mary Firestone (Bridgestone Books, 2003).
- *Picnic* by Chris Baines and Penny Ives (Frances Lincoln, Ltd., 2000).
- *Picnic* by Emily Arnold McCully (HarperCollins, 2003).
- *Picnic at Mudsock Meadow* by Patricia Polacco (Putnam Juvenile, 1992).
- *A Picnic in October* by Eve Bunting (Voyager Books, 2004).
- *Pinky and Rex* by James Howe (Aladdin, 1998).
- *Pinky and Rex and the Just-Right Pet* by James Howe (Aladdin, 2002).
- *Planes* by Francesca Baines (Franklin Watts, Ltd., 2001).
- *Planes at the Airport* by Peter Mandel (Cartwheel, 2004).
- *Poppleton in Spring* by Cynthia Rylant (Blue Sky Press, 1999).

• —————————— • **R** • —————————— •

- *Rain* by Robert Kalan (HarperTrophy, 1991).
- *Rain* by Manya Stojic (Crown Books for Young Readers, 2000).
- *The Rain Came Down* by David Shannon (Blue Sky Press, 2000).
- *The Rain Forest* by Pat Malone (National Geographic Society, 2001).
- *Rain Romp: Stomping Away a Grand Day* by Jane Kurtz (Greenwillow Books, 2002).
- *Ronald Morgan Goes to Bat* by Patricia Giff (Puffin Books, 1990).

• —————————— • **S** • —————————— •

- *A Salmon for Simon* by Betty Waterton and Ann Blades (Groundwood Books, 1998).
- *Salmon Princess: An Alaska Cinderella Story* by Mindy Dwyer (Paws IV Publishing, 2004).
- *The Seasons of Arnold's Apple Tree* by Gail Gibbons (Voyager Books, 1989).
- *Should We Have Pets? A Persuasive Text* by Sylvia Loliss and Joyce Hogan (Mondo Publishing, 2002).
- *Sleeping Over* by Melinda Beth Radabaugh (Heinemann Library, 2002).

- *The Sleepover Journal: A Light-Pen Diary* by Jon Kauffman (Chronicle Books, 2002).
- *Smoky Night* by Eve Bunting (Voyager Books, 1999).
- *The Snow Bear* by Miriam Moss (Dutton Juvenile, 2001).
- *Snow Dance* by Lezlie Evans (Houghton Mifflin Company, 1997).
- *Snow Is Falling* by Franklyn M. Branley (HarperTrophy, 2000).
- *The Snowy Day* by Ezra Jack Keats (Puffin Books, 1976).
- *Soccer Sam* by Jean Marzollo (Random House Books for Young Readers, 1987).
- *Splish, Splash, Spring* by Jan Carr (Holiday House, 2002).
- *Stella, Queen of the Snow* by Marie-Louise Gay (Scholastic, Inc., 2000).
- *The Stupids Take Off* by Harry G. Allard (Houghton Mifflin Company, 1993).
- *Swimmy* by Leo Lionni (Dragonfly Books, 1973).

• ———————— • T • ————————— •

- *Thomas Goes Fishing* by the Reverend W. Awdry (Random House Books for Young Readers, 2005).
- *Three Cheers for Tacky* by Helen Lester (Houghton Mifflin Company, 1996).
- *The Tiny Seed* by Eric Carle (Aladdin, 2001).
- *Trapped in the Museum of Unnatural History* by Dan Greenburg (Rebound by Sagebrush, 2002).

• ———————— • U • ————————— •

- *Up, Up, Up! It's Apple-Picking Time* by Jody Fickes Shapiro (Holiday House, 2003).
- *Using Math to Fly a Jumbo Jet* by Wendy and David Clemson (Gareth Stevens Publishing, 2004).

• ———————— • V • ————————— •

- *Visiting the Art Museum* by Laurene Kransy Brown and Marc Brown (Puffin Books, 1992).

• ———————— • W • ————————— •

- *Wackiest White House Pets* by Gibbs Davis (Scholastic Press, 2004).
- *We Just Moved!* by Stephen Krensk (Cartwheel, 1998).
- *We're Going on a Picnic!* by Pat Hutchins (Greenwillow Books, 2002).
- *We're Going to the Zoo* by Lorraine Gallacher (Simon Spotlight/Nickelodeon, 2001).
- *What Is a Fish?* by Robert Snedden (Sierra Club Books for Children, 1997).
- *What to Expect When You Go to the Dentist* by Heidi E. Murkoff (HarperFestival, 2002).
- *What's It Like to Be a Fish?* by Wendy Pfeffer (HarperTrophy, 1996).
- *Wheels on the Bus* by Paul O. Zelinski (Orchard Books, 2002).

REFERENCES

- *When I See My Dentist* by Susan Kuklin (Simon & Schuster Children's Publishing, 1988).
- *When the Rain Comes* by Marilyn Woolley (National Geographic Society, 2001).
- *When We Go Camping* by Margreit Ruurs (Tundra Books, 2001).
- *Where Does the Water Go?* by Mario Lucca (National Geographic Society, 2001).
- *Where the River Begins* by Thomas Locker (Puffin Books, 1993).
- *Wildfire!* by Annie Auerbach (Little Simon, 2004).
- *Winter Visitors* by Elizabeth Lee O'Donnell (HarperCollins Publishers, 1997).
- *Working at a Museum* by Arthur John L'Hommedieu (Children's Press, 1999).
- *Wow! City!* by Robert Neubecker (Hyperion, 2004).

• —————————————— • **Y** • —————————————— •

- *Young Cam Jansen and the Baseball Mystery* by David A. Adler (Puffin Books, 2001).
- *Young Cam Jansen and the Double Beach Mystery* by David A. Adler (Puffin Books, 2003).
- *Young Cam Jansen and the Lost Tooth* by David A. Adler (Puffin Books, 1999).
- *Young Cam Jansen and the Zoo Note Mystery* by David A. Adler (Puffin Books, 2004).

• —————————————— • **Z** • —————————————— •

- *Zoo-Looking* by Mem Fox (Mondo Publishing, 1996).

METRIC CONVERSIONS

Measurement Equivalents: Standard = Metric

- ½ teaspoon = 2.5 ml
- 1 teaspoon = 5 ml
- 1 tablespoon = 15 ml
- 1 fluid ounce = 30 ml
- ¼ cup = 60 ml
- ½ cup = 120 ml
- ⅔ cup = 160 ml
- 1 cup = 240 ml
- 2 cups = 475 ml
- 1 quart = 1 liter
- ½ gallon = 2 liter
- ½ inch = 1.25 cm
- ¾ inch = 2 cm
- 1 inch = 2.5 cm

Oven Temperature Equivalents: Fahrenheit = Celsius*

- 350° F = 180° C
- 375° F = 190° C
- 400° F = 200° C
- 425° F = 220° C

*When cooking above 160° C with an electric oven, increase the Celsius setting 10 to 20 degrees.